AIRDRIE

Recollections of an Artist in Bloom by
MARGOT MCMAHON

[signature: Margot Mc Mahon]

AQUARIUS PRESS
Detroit, Michigan

AIRDRIE
Recollections of an Artist in Bloom
© 2021 by Margot McMahon

978-1-7367677-7-1

Library of Congress Control Number: 2021939298

Disclaimer: This book is based upon the author's own personal and familial recollections.

Cover art: "Airdrie," (c) 2021 Margot McMahon

Credits: Parts of *AIRDIRE* first appeared in *If Trees Could Talk*, the second book in a trilogy about Margot's family in Chicago and Ireland.

AQUARIUS PRESS, www.AquariusPress.net

info@MargotMcMahon.com

Printed in the United States of America

Contents

For all young artists in bloom:
Grace the world with your talents and be kind to the Earth.

Sketches

Autumn

Socks. They seemed to be the main reason for varying levels of raucous arguments. Stockings, garters, lace anklets, Sunday shoes and muffs were searched for in a flurry of thunderous scrambling upstairs. We were too young to watch over those younger than us. "Where did you put it?", "Those are mine!" and "Oh no, one stocking has a run! Can I borrow one?" churned from bedrooms. Dad was already up. He'd wake early every morning, very early, to get out of bed at 5:00 a.m. If the cat *meAAAAWWWEdd!* at 3 a.m., he was up for the night, after having tossed the cat over the bedroom balcony. That's when he became quieter. *Why take it out on the cat?* That Sunday morning, he was at the kitchen table, reading *The New Yorker*, sipping black coffee and crunching wheat toast with orange marmalade. That's the way it was.

"Is the cat okay?" I asked Dad.

His eyebrows seemed to say, *That cat woke me up!* "Cats' legs are made to spring if they fall out of trees, she'll be okay," Dad said. He went out to warm up the van in the courtyard for Mass. Thunderous footsteps cascaded down the grand front stairs. Orange juice and milk were consumed on the fly as we tumbled out the portico door from the kitchen. "Off we go, into the wild blue yonder, flying high into the sky..." we all sang sleepy and slow as the van passed through the front gates.

Under certain circumstances, there is no other day more desirable than Sunday. The Lord's Day, a day of rest, Communion and dinner with family. On this particularly splendid spring morning, a red-tailed hawk soared with the Lake Michigan breezes and altocumulus clouds over the shoreline, up the steep cliff to cast widespread wing shadows over a stately home with its back to the lake. Leaded, slightly open windows reflected the flight. In the center of a first floor bay of windows is a double door overlooking a long wide carpet of a wide lawn. This bay offered a morning sun to warm our grandmother where she sat during her weekly visit. The hawk flapped its wings beside the chimney to land on a branch of a grand old oak over the courtyard as the Volkswagen van wound its way through the maple and oak forest onto Mayflower Road.

This house is named Airdrie and we were its second family. Capped with arched terra cotta tiles, the stucco walls stood facing an acre of trees secluding it from Mayflower Road. Lined with windows facing east, Airdrie gestured westward to a winding drive through a forest that bowed, in the breeze, to the grand old oak in its courtyard. The springtime fragrance of tulips and forsythia, summer lake breezes and fall burning leaves created an air of expectation for Gramma Mac's large brown Packard to park under the oak on Sundays. Later in the day, our Volkswagen van re-entered the narrow gate barely containing a boisterous family of eleven returning home from St. Mary's Mass.

"Why are you arguing? Be glad you have each other," Dad said.

Called "Mac" by family and friends, our father quietly exited the driver's door with two newspapers under his arm. He was intent on an agenda he'd laid out during the quiet moments of Mass. The world knows him as William Franklin McMahon, nationally-awarded artist-reporter. Broad-shouldered, six-foot-three-inches tall, with dark hair thinning from a rounded crown, he strode purposefully to the front door with a serious expression on his clean-shaven face. The van's side door slid open and four boys in penny loafers, blue uniform slacks, white shirts and loosened clip-ties leapt out. The third of four girls, I was lucky number seven; I jumped, with black patent leather shoes and lacy white bobby socks, into the thick pea gravel to make two divots. Three girls followed. The oldest lifted the youngest to the ground. Their shouts exploded upon their escape from the crowded van and eternally long Mass. Turtle candies, tiny green army men with parachutes, balsa wood planes, rolls of black and white film and a paper kite purchased at Walgreens® drug store were clutched in our hands.

"Grandma will be coming soon!" said our mother. She wore a fashionable paisley dress and matching high heels. Her community knew her as generous, caring and insightful. "Change into play clothes. Supper will be served at three. Roast-a Beef-a at three!"

Inside Airdrie's eclectic Spanish-style courtyard sat the dark-paneled home, both grand and comfortable. Tall ceilings over hand-plastered walls and dark-stained oak paneling were graced with art pieces collected from world travels of both the current and previous owners. A leaded glass star fixture hung in the bay door that led to the expansive back lawn. Two stuffed tea chairs and a table filled the sunny bay. A *New Yorker* magazine was set on the table, awaiting our Grandmother's visit. I joined my little brother and sister, in pedal pushers, and we sat around the strewn newspaper sections and couch pillows, on a very long couch that faced an oak fireplace, embers figuring out what to play.

We jumped on the couch springs like it was a trampoline. Then pillows were arranged into cells, separate forts facing the fireplace. We looked into the fireplace flames and rattled on from our imaginary world.

~

Dad stepped into the foyer where two sons competed to fly their balsa wood planes further.

"Pilots, Set?" he called.

"Set!" they called.

One plane rose and crashed. The other glided into the living room. Dad quietly stopped to bend up the tips of the wings and adjusted a metal crimp on the front of fuselage. "Winds" and the "lift" of heavy things was in our vocabulary. Through the bay doors and across and the expansive lawn, children ran with a twisting, twirling kite that nosedived into the uncut grass. Dad stepped out of the door onto the brick patio. A plastic parachute hovered and a tiny green army man drifted towards him from the balcony.

"Hey Dad, please throw him back up!" Hugh called. Dad twisted the parachute around the tiny soldier and tossed the toy up to a catching set of hands. It took two tries.

Dad, at the end of the lawn, held the nearly broken paper kite.

"Get a thin cotton rag from the laundry room." He slid the tethering bowed string to a one-third position on the harnessing string. A thin strip of old sheet was ripped and tied on the bottom for a tail. The kite still dipped in the strong wind off the lake. Two more strips were tied to the pointed tail end. Patrick held the kite while Elizabeth ran into the wind. The kite flew! By pumping the string, the kite rose and dropped until it caught an updraft from the steep cliff and shot into space. Cheers erupted until the steadily dancing kite was barely visible in the clouds.

"Dad! Gram's here!" I called from the bay door. Sheba was barking.

Dad hurried up the acre of lawn. The hawk rose from the branch and flew over the lawn shadowing Dad as it glided out to the lake. He entered the bay door. His three youngest children were sitting crossed-legged in side-by-side cells built of slumping couch pillows. Dad loved a hearth fire and always had one burning in his grand fireplace. He looked away with a we-were-only-playing look as we carried on in our imaginary world. Dad circled the tea table with the *New Yorker* and greeted Gram with a reassuring hug in the dark foyer. The dog barked incessantly.

Mom was picking up the balsa wood plane shards that lay splintered on the Iranian rug.

"Please put the pillows back, your grandmother is here," she said while untying her apron. The barking did not stop. Mom rang the dinner bell. Stomping clamored down the front hall as our family gathered from bedrooms, forests and lawns. Dad and Gram sat at the afternoon dinner table with twelve blue-eyed McMahons and recited "Bless us, O Lord, and these, thy gifts, which we are about to receive from your bounty through Christ, Our Lord…" over interlocked fingers. The table was a length of laminated wood cut from the Lake Forest Bowling alley that closed the previous year. The long length still showed the dings and divots from dropped bowling balls. A collection of press-backed chairs with cane-woven seats circled the table. The five-door black and-white oven had a series of recently used and nearly empty pots on its eight-burner gas range.

"Amen," we all ended with a clatter of forks.

I don't remember mirrors in my childhood home. I'd had no image of myself beyond my reflection in ten family members circling the kitchen table. What I knew was: Silver-haired Mom, Irene, sat at the refrigerator end, with curly-haired John in a high chair to her left side. By the stove, ebony-haired Jean, Elizabeth, and Hugh. Chestnut-haired Dad, and Frank on the other end, then on the side, Andrew, me and Mary, auburn-tipped Patrick sat. All had blue eyes. Half, but not all boys, were left-handed and the youngest was ambidextrous. Our birth years stretched three decades. Less than half saved the tip of their pie slice for last to make a wish. It seemed family dinners would continue like this forever. Yet, change was inevitable.

I yearned to be seven again. We were under the same roof in 1963. We flowed together like a flock of birds. We still had a promising future led by the first Irish Catholic president. Our mother guided us loosely according to patterns set before I was born. When my unknown grandfather died, Gramma Mac abruptly moved to California, which ended her Sunday visits. My two oldest brothers went to boarding school that fall, which started the peeling off of a sister or brother every year for college.

"Please pass the mashed potatoes," Gram said over the long kitchen table. The morning rain from Chicago had followed her thirty-five miles north to patter against the darkened windows.

"Why do that to a potato?" Dad joked as he spooned the steaming mound onto his plate. "JFK plans to launch Ranger 7 this summer. I just heard from the *Tribune*. I'll go to Cape Canaveral and cover its take-off."

"Oh Franklin, that's very exciting!" Gram said. "You'll paint a remarkable work."

"When is the launch?" Mom asked.

"July. So I need to book flights now," Dad said.

"What will Ranger do in space?" a brother asked.

"This mission is to take television photographs of the moon's surface," Dad said. "NASA is interested in finding out about the dark shadows of the moon. To see what they are."

"Bess, do you want some apple pie?" Mom asked as she carried a plate to Gram and hoped to change the subject. She stayed grounded while Dad painted the excitement of the space race. Would you like more ice cream?"

"Can I be excused?" Patrick asked, making a wish as he finished his pie tip.

"Yes, you can," Mom replied.

"Me too?" chimed Elizabeth, Mary, and Frank.

They got Dad's nod.

"How will you draw the spaceship taking off?" a brother asked. "Won't it go too fast?"

"I plan to get there a day or two in advance and draw the scene," Dad said. "Then, on the launch day, I fill in the people and the action." Over the clatter of forks, half of the family made a silent wish with their last piece of pie. The revolving door spun in for a full house at summer, and out for echoing halls seasonally. They never really came home again. I adjusted to the unraveling of us, as they moved into different lives.

~

A single warbling thrush repeated its song as the day began to glow. When I was five, I woke up early in the quiet of morning, looking through my eight-framed, second-story window at a red sunrise over the lake, through a three-story cherry tree canopy. Chirruping, trilling, then a quavering chorus of birds cheeping and twittering filled the warming air. The rising red, then orange ball made a pointillist reflective path that skimmed over the water straight to me. Each frame of the window offered a new composition of stark, purpled-brown branches against a blue sky with the backlighting of a new day's early spring sun. If I shifted slightly, I could change the arrangement of wintery branches within the glass pane. For hours, I composed this tree. The spaces between the branches took the shapes of dragons and unicorns that moved as the clouds blew past. As the windowpanes warmed with encroaching spring, buds emerged and burst into fragile pink blossoms that consumed the dark branches. The blossoms clung to the branch in clusters of five. Sawtooth-edged, shiny green leaves made a dappled shade to cool the warming air. The breeze flipped up a downy underside. The sun burned white hot making liquid silver paths on the lake, then dots and dashes of watery reflections as Mary stirred in the next bed. Over the weeks, one petal at a time dropped as light green spring leaves unfurled to new arrangements. Each year, these leaves turned pink, then orange, then cherry red before dropping out of the frames of my window. As I composed a falling red leaf before a clear blue sky, my mother's high heels could be heard on the long wooden hallway.

"Arriba! Arriba!" she called and the house started to grumble for Mass. "Sunday Mass in half hour." A long hall of snores became a rumble.

"Sky's the limit!" our mother cheered us on over a quick cereal breakfast. Dad and Mom kissed goodbye as he drove to the train. She put on a coat to drive me to my first day of kindergarten. If everything you need in life is learned in kindergarten, mine was an adventure. Mom and I talked as she drove along Sheridan Road. I clicked my new brown Hush Puppies saddle shoes that stuck straight out from the back seat. She and I entered Gorton's east door, past the auditorium to a cozy classroom. My first day of kindergarten began with my little hand in Mom's graceful one.

"You'll be with your classmates for a while. I'll pick you up for lunch." Our hands dropped their hold. I gaped wide-eyed at children crying and comforted by strangers.

"Why are they all crying?" I turned to my mother. She was gone. I sobbed. A stranger helped me hang my coat under a square that told the day in the week with felt symbols for weather underneath. She asked me what the day was like? "Sunny," I responded. I was shown how to peel off the round yellow felt sun with spiky edges and place it on *Monday* in rainbow colors above a row of cubbies. Painting with too-thick brushes on a papered easel, I set out to compose the cherry tree in my framed bedroom window. Blossoms scattered along black cherry branches, against a blue sky. Then I remembered the sunrise and dipped a new brush in red. The brush was raised to dab…

"What a lovely painting!" a teacher said too loud. My brush pushed into the paper and the red paint dripped.

"Oh my!" she exclaimed, flustered and upset. *Why was she scurrying about?* I stared at my ruined image, the dripping brush. She pointed to the piddle between my new saddle-shoes. *I had no idea where that came from? Did something spill? Was I too focused?*

"I don't know where it came from?" I said.

"I'll send your painting home when it dries," she said to my glance back as I was whisked to the office. Thick padded undies and a plastic bag were handed to me. I changed into the novel padded pair and went home in Mom's car full of silence. Why was she quiet? I never returned to Gorton.

I started kindergarten again at my sister's Catholic school. I would have picked a cloudy felt image and put it on Tuesday's square at my first school. After buttoning a Peter-Pan collared white blouse, and safety pinning on a too-big plaid skirt. After fourteen shoes laces were tied, eleven sets of teeth and seven heads brushed, faces washed, nine bowls of cereal were eaten, two with coffee. Seven sandwiches, with apples and chips, were in brown paper bags when Mom cheered, "Don't take any wooden nickels!" My four brothers in blue pants and white shirts and two skirted sisters led me to the bus stop a long block from home. The bus opened the door in the girl's playground near the marble of St. Mary's.

My too-tight pigtails pulled as I was introduced to my teacher who looked Muslim in a long black draping habit with a tight white headband and veil below-her-shoulders like women in Spain, until we recited, "Hail Mary, full of grace the Lord is with thee, Blessed art thou amongst women..." We were led behind her flowing habit in a line down a dark hallway when a loud buzzer sounded. We sat along the wall hugging our knees that slipped out of plaid skirts and showed our navy knee socks while nuns locked the windows tight to keep out nuclear air if a missile reached Chicago from Cuba.

Back in the classroom, a boy sat facing the corner wearing a pointed red hat that had large letters, DUNCE, while we filed out to play. Mom looked hard at me when I told her about it at dinner. Silence followed. I didn't return to the Catholic school, either.

Rain trickled down the window to my third kindergarten at Sheridan School. I would have placed a felt rain under a grey cloud symbol under the Wednesday square two kindergartens ago. Two large-windowed kindergarten rooms had an art studio with four walls of windows between them. I rushed through my schoolwork so I could roll snakes and punch my tiny fingers into soft clay. Thursday and Friday would have been sunshine symbols as I hurried through my schoolwork to work with clay. *Was this school chosen for me to discover who I was an artist? I'll never know.*

~

On Saturday, Dad lifted me up onto the window seat

in the end bay window of his studio. I had padded into his studio with my pink bunny slippers. He was painting with encaustics, a mixture of pigment in hot wax.

"Please take those off," he said. I put the slippers on the seat next to me after being careful not to roll off the soft ledge. Dad's hand, with his wrist at a vertical right angle, held a long paintbrush up above a pot of hot wax. Turpentine and Damar Varnish fumes drifted into the two-story room. Above him was lit a large suspended white globe fixture.

"Will you paint my bunny slippers too?" I asked, disappointed in his silence. I sat very still hoping the slippers might be painted into the seat. He squeezed paint onto a palette dripped on some oil, mixed it with a wrist holding a paintbrush horizontally. It was a pointy paintbrush and the titanium white blob now had a bit of cadmium red in it on one side, some thalo blue on another side. *Would they make pink?* I waited even longer while trying not to fall asleep. I didn't want to fall from up high. I concentrated on how he might make the softness, the light pink color, the little ears with white centers.

"So, how's the bunny slippers going?" I quietly asked.

"I am not going to paint in those bunny slippers." He was agitated now. I slumped, forlorn, wondering what else would he paint? He was trying hard to get something right. I watched him struggle to make it just so. Maybe he was happy when he said it was enough for the day. I wandered out but he kept painting.

Another day, I sat again. I didn't bring the slippers. I could tell he was relieved. His tall easel was set so I couldn't see what he was working on. He went back and forth with a brush or two in his mouth and a couple of them in his hands. He wiped something off with an old T-shirt rag. Oil paint filled my nose and a sneeze exploded. We didn't talk. With only eyes moving, I looked around the studio with its tall ceiling and giant glass doors. I looked through them at the magnolia tree and the lake. A giant fireplace was on my left side in an alcove. The double doors to my left looked out to Mom's impatiens garden shaded by the oak tree. The heel of my socks caught in the metal screens covering the radiator. My arms flew up to keep me on my perch. Dad reached out. I gained my balance. Stiff-necked, I looked forward.

I didn't want to be older, just seven my whole life. I'd cross paths with my Dad at the bottom of Airdrie's front steps, he'd lift me onto his toes and we'd dance the tango on the Iranian rug in the front foyer. Passing in the hall he'd show a few boxing steps and teach a fake undercut to the chin. That's when my grandmother still lived in Chicago. That was before my brothers left for boarding school. Everything once was whole and intact. We were busy every day and what was experienced by one of us, was felt by all of us. We all strove to be together and fiercely struggled for our parent's attention, a chair in the TV room and second servings. The organism that was *us* moved like a swirling flock of swallows in unison as we shifted with needs, hurts and wants. Dad raised us with a few well-chosen words and a silent observer's eye. Mom created peace by flat-lining favoritism, never arguing with Dad and making a steady structure based on age. Boys had outdoor chores and girls indoors. Everyone did their laundry and the dishes in pecking order. Beds were made with military corners and teeth brushed before breakfast and bedtime. The straggler was given more one-on-one time at the kitchen table drilling math or spelling. The ever-present canopy of Mom's watchful eye allowed us to reach for the sky in her shadow.

"That's my chair!" was called out from behind as we watched the black and white skinny panther who solved the mystery for a missing diamond. Rows of wicker chairs diagonally filled the linen closet room. Cupboards lined the walls with shelves and drawers of sheets and pillows, towels and plastic baskets. The chair before me blocked half the small screen, the chair behind scratched the wooden floor while Jacques Clouseau inspected a door handle.

"No one was here when I came."

"I called 'Saved!'" Two windows reverberated the shouts in the small room. Nine seats barely fit. Jacques Clouseau's mystery was solved and the diamond was replaced in the museum. Mr. Maggoo and his suitcase scuttled into the small TV screen. I walked out, down the wide creaky front stairs and opened the heavy front door. The door closed.

Rustling leaves, bird songs and darting colors filled the air. Forsythia and tulips lined the stucco walls with early smells of spring. A bright orange bird flickered down from the oak, darted into the woods. I ran after it. It disappeared in the bright green canopy. Beneath the branches were yellow trumpets and white pointed flowers carpeting beneath the brush. Layers of plants and colors. Darting birds, mosquitos and spiders were everywhere. A web glistened with dew. A spider scurried. I walked further down the middle path and saw green cones bent over with lined vertically striped leaves. Surrounded by flashes of color on all sides, I called "Saved." No one argued in the front woods.

~

I started first grade. "Good Morning Sister Mary Michaelina!" In plaid uniforms, we stood and chanted before our morning *Hail Mary* prayer with palms pressed together and fingers pointed up. After living in three homes, two countries and having gone to three kindergartens, I settled in for eight years at St. Mary's in a brand-new uniform skirt and sweater. We recited, the *Pledge of Allegiance of the United States* with our right hand pressed over our heart. "...One nation under God, for liberty and justice for all." In class, we recited "We the people, in order to form a more perfect union...". At home, we chanted, "We shall overcome." While my parents planned their round-the-world trip, Sister Mary Michaelina led us single file to the art room to make resin angel sculptures for Christmas.

When Mom and Dad were on the other side of the world, School Principal, Sister Davide, announced through sobs on the P.A. system that we were all being sent home by bus early. President Kennedy had just been shot. The nun's responses were frightening. They cried. They turned red faced. They yelled. They rushed us out of school to a bus through the bleak, steady, torrential November rain to our sitter, Mrs. Christianson, sobbing in front of the television. At dinner, she took a sip from a JFK coffee cup and choked uncontrollably. We were all sent to our rooms. Apologetically, she called down for Oreos and milk. The rain did not stop. We were sent back to our rooms gently.

I ached for Mom's patterns. She didn't cry. She didn't send us to our rooms. Outdoors, yes, but not to our rooms. Suddenly, I became aware of Mom's patterns. While we were a cohesive Roman Catholic family practicing a weekly structure, each of us whorled and wove our individual definitions. Thank God she came home early from her world tour. She gathered us around to unpack boxed Japanese dolls with six interchangeable hair pieces and wooden shoes. The boys were given printed blue fish kites made of cotton cloth tubes on poles. Dolls from Amsterdam, France, Germany and Italy were unwrapped and placed on living room shelves next to the bay window. Dad returned home later with a Japanese brush stroke movement to ink his drawings. His fingers pointing straight down to a brush, from a bent wrist. The ink, pulled by gravity to the brush tip, swirled by his wrist to express direct confident lines. We were not told his father had died and he returned early to bury him.

Gramma Mac took us three girls to the Barnum and Bailey circus. It seemed a rite of passage and important to her that we have this experience. Tigers jumping through hoops of fire, clowns peddling unicycles with striped clothes, elephants parading from largest to smallest and a myriad of costumed chimpanzees that made us laugh. She took two of us to the fireworks on the 4th of July before we didn't see her for months. She called Dad to say she was visiting a friend in California. She called again to say she had bought a car. She called again to say she was married again.

"Jack O'Connor." Dad told Mom. "Mother married her high school boyfriend."

~

"Mom, what's Dad's favorite color?" I asked as dusk settled. The yellow kitchen glowed with the smells of stuffed peppers and lima beans. Mom was tearing iceberg lettuce into a salad. Chives speckled sliced tomatoes.

21

"Why don't you ask him? It's time for dinner, please let your Dad know." Passing the portico door into the mudroom, I paused where the TV was flickering *Hogan's Heroes* on my brother's and sister's faces in the waning light. A sister, at the long picnic table, was making a light drawing, plugging color pegs into a light box, with a Lite Brite. Her face was side lit by the TV, but around her nose reflected many colors from the pegs.

A series of cupboards on the left had art kits and toys gifted by Santa Claus at the annual Artist Guild Small Fry Show. I passed the dark dining room opposite the front staircase, through the front foyer and living room into a narrow hall. Dad's darkly paneled dim office with a fireplace and desk by a courtyard window opened to a two-story high white stucco room with the effect of being outside at sunset. I silently stepped down two broad stairs with bare feet through a spacious lofty room filled with artwork. Dad was hovering a painting over a single burner, melting brush marks into a layer of wax.

"I like the trees," I said.

"Thank you. What do you like about them?"

"The branches are like lots of spider webs. What is your favorite color?"

"Oh I don't know. I like all colors," he said.

"Which one do you like most?" I watched him add oil paint to the wax pool.

"The color to finish my painting."

"How is it that every kid in my class knows their favorite color and you don't have a favorite color?" I said.

After dinner, dishes washed, music practiced, homework

22

completed, Mary and I took turns filling the bath when Dad appeared to say goodnight. A centipede crawled in the porcelain sink. "Dad, its gigantic!" I cried out with wide eyes. Shaking out his pocket kerchief he carefully scooped it.

"Let's give it a chance to live." He lifted the squirming bug outside to the window ledge, set it down and cranked the window closed. "I changed my mind, my favorite color is the color of your eyes."

~

Though Mom's dream of raising nine children was more than two full time jobs, she had traversed the country by propeller plane, been a community organizer, had a degree to teach art, and was certified in Montessori. She had grown up in Our Lady of Sorrows Catholic Parish, where she envied large families. She missed her racially and religiously diverse childhood with heaps of kids in the neighborhood. When John, her ninth child, started first grade, Mom volunteered at a Catholic Church in Bronzeville. On Tuesdays, she and her grassroots friends commuted to the Southside to teach reading and math with Montessori methods. Head Start or social programs were not yet extant. They drove along the Dan Ryan knowing the Black Stone Rangers ruled, knowing the kids they'd teach witnessed violence. They entered the Church back door and stepped down to the basement.

"Did you hear what happened last night?" a student from Ida B. Wells asked when they entered. The volunteers let them talk about the shooting, who was killed, what teen was pregnant, and what the Black Stone Rangers did after dark. They showed bruises on their arms from an uncle who got too close. These women listened and parented, until one student would say, "Our parents want us to learn, we want to learn, let's forget what happened for a while. These women have come to help us." Still in winter coats and with gloves on, they wrote their names in script, solved math problems and turned pages of a book in an unheated church.

Dad's latest brown paper packages slumped, with worn edges and torn corners, behind his pressed back chair. After our stories of getting detention for bangs in our eyes or a dislocated shoulder at volleyball, Dad's images of historic moments on heavy paper, captured by a veri-black pencil and watercolor paint, brought home the gestures and likenesses of Eisenhower and Goldwater, JFK's funeral, MLK 's freedom speech, LBJ's mutual contempt with Bobby Kennedy. He explained the speeches while showing paintings from "a guy like Babbit, or Dukakis, or Mondale or McGovern who didn't make it." Before dessert, Dad would lift one drawing from the package. What came out, one at a time, was a World's Fair of contemporary images of injustice not seen yet in *our* nation's heartland: religion, race, economy, segregation, women's rights, health, environment, housing and education. We saw paintings of barefoot boys playing soccer in Egypt or the Ayres Rock in Australia, a bamboo scaffold used to build skyscrapers in China and Japanese letters in neon lights in Tokyo. He would show us about the Bishops Synod of Vatican II in Rome, Robert Kennedy's ambition, Martin Luther King or a Continental Bank in London. We learned compound words: *Embrace ecumenical; We shall overcome; Ave Maria.* He showed us the poverty and wonders of the world through pencil on paper and told us stories of what it was like to be there. He gave us an international understanding that inspired world peace and a wonder about other religions and customs.

History and solutions came to life as Dad described the Korean War, the Bay of Pigs and the Civil Rights Movement. President Johnson's War on Poverty with Head Start, Legal Aid, VISTA and then the Peace Corps were explained with his infectious excitement. I was in school the day he covered the Marquette Park riots, but know the event from our dinner conversations. I experienced it through Dad's art and heard the stories that became confusing when I jumped rope at St. Mary's girls' playground. "Daisy give me you answer true. It won't be a stylish marriage, but you'd look sweet upon the seat of a bicycle built for two." We talked about crushes with boys while I struggled internally about recent protests. If it was his experience, told with imagery, was it my experience too?

"Sticks and Stones may break my bones, but names will never hurt me," we sang as we jumped rope. Growing up in Catholic Schools during Vatican II was watching adults undergoing profound personal change of beliefs as if our noses were pressed against glass, frosted by the hurried breath of change. While I was learning to read and add, St. Mary's Sisters of Mercy wore full habits and were decreed by Pope Benedict to meet each other. Nuns resisted, stating they had made vows of being cloistered. The girls in my class toured the convent to see sparse tiny cells, a tidy twin bed with one dresser and a closet. Pope Benedict demanded nuns meet at a conference. Mercy in heaven! Once they met no one could stop them! One nun may have stopped wearing her veil or looping a rosary through her belt. As the years progressed

nuns shed their habits, one bit at a time, for blouses, pumps and a hair style in a flip. The world had not yet met a country of women who only took care of children six hours a day. They led civil rights marches and their pledge to Jesus included housing and medicating the poor while feeding the hungry. The old guard dug in their worn heels in the convent. We saw and felt the discourse in the classroom. Dad painted the Irish Catholic Kennedys and walked on water at school. Nuns treated me with respect owed to him and glorified him beyond a mere father. Teachers asked me for his autograph. He walked by silently. When I bumped into Dad in the front hall, rather than dancing the Tango like three years ago, I could barely say hello.

~

Mom and Dad went to report on the peaceful Selma-Montgomery march and the John F Kennedy Space Center

Gemini Program launch. With a press pass, Dad joined his Catholic clergy friends to drop into Selma to draw this moment of history. Mom's empathy gave her the courage to let him go, then decided to join him. March 7, 1965, the television penetrated into our home showing the Edmund Pettus Bridge police massacre of peaceful southern protestors who wanted to vote. Police on horseback chased unarmed, elderly women and children, beating them with bully sticks. They were there to terrify, but the sticks cracked skulls. We watched the protestors herded into a black enclave of three brick churches and a row of public housing. Dad heard that protestors escaped into a church only to have firecrackers thrown through the windows by police. An older woman who fell in the melee had a lighted cigarette burnt against her buttock. Children were left home alone while adults were hospitalized or jailed.

Monday night, a young Unitarian divinity student who was active in enabling black voter registration was cornered and beaten to death. Monsignor Egan made it clear that no clergy was to step outside alone and without their collar or habit intact. Within the circle of the Catholic clergy, Dad created a safe, protected corner to draw the Civil Rights Movement while Mom wrote her impressions. By Wednesday night, he was in a church jam-packed with civil rights characters and locals. They held hands in the cross-breasted custom with laborers who had broken hands and slinged arms to sing "We Shall Overcome." At Holy Communion, Dad was moved by the protected white cleric with smooth and scholarly palms, connecting to the brave working man who wore bib overalls and denim. Thursday, Friday, and Saturday, the days blurred.

Dr. King did not come until Monday or Tuesday, but everyone else was there, staying in houses and apartments, being fed by traumatized young teenagers whose parents and grandparents were hospitalized or jailed. There were many meetings for careful planning of the next march. Dad was fascinated with the intense basement planning meetings with crucifixes glinting at the end of rosaries. Archbishop Iakovos appeared on the altar-platform of the church for one of the rallies of song and inspirational witness. The crossed arms were tricky for him, as he propped his Archiepiscopal Staff in a bobbling arrangement between his elbow while swaying back and forth. Dad told me he was grinning, as if no liturgy he had ever known was as wild and as much fun as this one. A beautiful sight in his tall crown and veil, and a worthy successor to the Apostles. Sunday, Dad watched small groups that went out to attend services in local churches, but were blocked from entering. They knelt on the pavement outside for prayers. Dr. King came and inspired the clergy, northern protestors, southerners hoping for voting rights, children, grandparents, angels and archangels and all the company of Heaven. Dad joined the masses that gathered and sang "*Holy, Holy, Holy is the Lord of Hosts. The whole earth is filled with his glory!*" He was careful to draw from a corner to not be noticed.

At dinner, Dad told us about being on a bus full of singing and shouting demonstrators in Montgomery. Outside, a group of southern white men, carrying flames, started to rock the bus. Dad stood up, raised his hands and calmly reasoned with the Northern protestors to stop singing. They quieted. The rocking of the bus subsided. The perpetrators moved on and the driver hurried away. "Forgive us our trespasses as we forgive those that trespass against us." Mom and Dad published an article about the Gemini Program space launch that was testing two astronauts, Gus Grissom and John Young as they orbited the earth three times tweaking their direction by firing thrusters and presenting the question if we could do that on earth with the voting rights act. My family was held tightly together by that strife that loomed outside our Airdrie's walls.

~

Winter

Holidays began with Halloween. Autumn's splendor and glory brazenly warded off insect and disease invaders with orange, red and yellow leaves as angled sun beams pierced our blue eyes. We burnt wine corks with matches to smudge our faces with hobo moustaches or witch's eyebrows, sewed patches on blazers or dressed all in black. With pillowcases in hand we set off to knock on mansion doors, deep in old oak woods at the end of long winding driveways. Knocking on very tall doors with dark windows was scary enough. One neighbor required we perform a trick, like a cartwheel or somersault, for a treat. "One hand only," another neighbor grinned, who offered a bowl of nickels. Mrs. French invited us in to walk around her dining room table of homemade brownies, popcorn balls, hot apple cider and cookies with her dozen cats circling our costumed feet.

We headed north on Mayflower, east on Deerpath, to Lake Street that ended at Lake Forest cemetery. Offshore wind in old oaks, creaked branches. An owl's hoot sent us running all the way home with our half-filled pillowcases knocking our backs and knees. In the linen room, we sorted our candy and traded until we slept deeply before waking with a traditional runny nose and cough. Five-foot-tall, white-haired Gram Leahy arrived in Airdrie's courtyard in her red Dodge Dart with a carload of Betty Crocker Cookbook treats: sandies; rice pudding; and shortbread. Gifts of knitted hats, crocheted slippers and tea pot cozies were unwrapped. Her charm bracelet jingled a comforting tune. Each etched round charm had one of her nineteen grandchildren's name and birthdate.

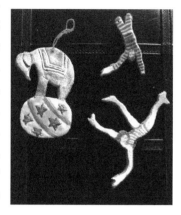

On Thanksgiving weekend, brothers and sisters returned from college. We squeezed around the mudroom table to halve potatoes and carve stars, trees, mangers, sleighs, in reverse for printing Christmas cards. The wet, freshly carved surface of the potato was tamped on a towel and pressed onto a stamp pad and folded card stock. Around Thanksgiving, a large box of tubed Container Corporation wrapping paper arrived from Walter Paepke. Mom and Aunt Mary Marg alternated holidays of hosting our potluck dinners with cousins.

"Let's do the razzle-dazzle play!" Dad always said in the huddle. Dads quarterbacked the kids for Turkey Bowl, then Santa Bowl and Bunny Bowl—touch-football with Uncle Harry and the Leahys opposing Dad and the McMahons. Razzle Dazzle had a lot of zig-zagging diagonally while the toss was mostly to the youngest player for first down. "Dinner!" called us in while the buffet was still steaming hot. The grandmothers fussed with a chocolate cake. Two sliced roasted turkeys, cranberries both jellied and sauced, herb stuffing, mashed potatoes with gravy, green beans, always Jello with embedded canned fruit in a ring mold shape. "Jello is good for the nails and bones," Gram Leahy said wanting all of us to be together. Gramma Mac handed all the cousins Kennedy half dollar coins.

On Christmas Eve, our eleven socks hung together from the mantle with care, clementines and walnuts stretching them into bulbous distortions. An evergreen, glittering with colored lights and metallic red, green and baked dough ornaments, stood in the bay window beneath the star light. We read Christmas poems and fables to each other, lit by a roaring fire before Midnight Mass. Every Christmas, Dad gifted Mom one-hundred single dollar bills in unique wrapping like glued pages of a hard-covered book that opened to a cut-out hollow filled with a stack of bills. The cousins came at three o'clock for Christmas dinner every other year. Spouses and great-grandchildren challenged even our ample homes for hosting until we cousins disbanded into two dinners.

Dad's stories and paintings evolved into films. A movie crew filmed his studio, panning across the cityscapes, crowds and events in his drawings to show how it felt to "be there." The active lines captured the energy of the room and the cadence of the music. Mom taped people's reflections to voice over impressions. In *American City at Christmas Time* Mom's captured sound and Dad's art tell of a dichotomous

cathedral mass blessing. Reverend Jesse Jackson chanted with prisoners in a jail, "I am somebody. I may be poor, I may be unemployed, but I am somebody! I am God's child" on Christmas Day. One Sunday evening after dinner, we all walked along the wooded path to the Harkin's home to watch Dad's film on a color television. We crowded around the giant color screen with built-in console speakers to watch Dad's first movie on WTTW that earned him a Peabody® Award. *Real Violins* captured the Chicago Symphony Orchestra becoming World Class by a tour through Europe then Japan, conducted by Sir George Solti. Dad transformed a room off the kitchen for *Rocinante Sight and Sound*, his film business. We watched his Emmy® award accepted on our black and white television not knowing where they had gone that night. Hooting and hollering exploded when his name was called as he rose to thank his wife and collaborators.

~

Spring

Annually, boxes of honey locust saplings arrived to signal spring. The rain softened the clay cliff so we could poke holes with broom poles to insert sprigs with a tapering root and kick-sealed hundreds of sprouts. Boxes emptied over the weeks of us traversing the slippery clay cliff under two to ten-year-old trees whose roots grew fast to hold the eroding bluff. At dusk, we descended a winding path of railroad ties held against pipes driven into the clay cliff for steps. Left above was the structure of school, clubs, sports, music lessons and patterns of meals with place settings and centerpieces. Down the cliff, time passed at the moon's pace of lapping waves and the changing tides as if the world ticked to the moon's pull. "Smelting is a Chicago tradition!" Dad made us part of Chicago's spring ritual as a driftwood bonfire crackled. After beaming flashlights into submerged nets, stretched into a square, squirming smelt were raised dripping at the end of a taught rope. Squiggly silver fish sprayed sweatshirts and pants letting the cold night seep in. "Bite the head off first!" a brother challenged. My stomach flipped. No one bit the head off, yet this chilly ritual call endured. Frying smelt sizzled in a cast iron pan on the sandy beach. The tide swelled towards the flames. Wet shoes were soaked by surf. Like the reflective moon dancing a path across the water, Mom presided with hot cider made in a large red kettle. Satisfied with our outdoor dinner, Dad directed us to the blinking constellations. Lazy bulbous clouds revealed strips of sky. He pointed out Orion's Belt, Cassiopeia, Taurus, twin fish of Pisces after spotting the Big Dipper and North Star in case we needed to find our way home. Weary, we climbed the cliff.

When Dad's loud whistle sounded, we'd alley-oop to line up like ducks into the Volkswagen van. My mother's pattern corralled us with *you don't ever want to miss a moment.* Once a year they'd take us to Arlington Park Race Track to make $2 bets. A philosophy of life was taught, to let go of a loss, to make a better guess for the next horse. Optimism was trained.

~

On a Saturday, pre-dawn, we all sleepily piled in the van for a tour of murals of Mexican heroes in Pilsen and Bronzeville. A mural was spotted, we woke up, saw walls covered with faces and names of admired neighbors and slept again. Pilsen's murals were colorful. We walked around Maxwell Street, one of the remaining industrial tool exchanges from Chicago past. I treasured my second-hand wood carving tools wrapped in cotton cloth. Dad showed us Henry Moore's *Nuclear Energy* dedicated above the Manhattan projects lab at the University of Chicago.

We drove around the Picasso sculpture at Daley Plaza at its unveiling. "It will rust superficially, sealing the surfaces of steel for hundreds of years." Dad said. We jumped out and ran up, slid down the inclined front while he circled the block. "Don't look in the warehouses," Dad said as we trekked around the stockyards of packing houses on 47th street. My curiosity led me to look in to see cows' rear hooves tied and hooked on a track, their necks bleeding black liquid into sandy dirt. A packing house worker looked concerned and closed the door. My stomach lurched. I tasted the smell of blood mixed with acrid smelling steel mill fumes from nearby and became vegetarian that day. We loaded in the van for *Man of La Mancha* who rode his horse Rocinate with a lance to conquer windmills for his beloved Dulcinea. The visual echoes of reality, images in mirrors of an idealistic man facing his own exuberance echoed in our belief to dream impossible dreams.

~

Careening through semis and slushy snow, ten families migrated south with the spring to a spit of sand called Santa Rosa Island off Florida's panhandle for spring break. Van's bulging with tents, books and beach gear squeezed through narrow gaps of tall trucks. The snow turned to rain as we raced to our overnight campground. Were we in Kentucky or Tennessee for gas fill up? "If we lose sight of you, we'll meet up in Florida," was said. The second day we opened our windows to the hot and humid smells of salt, palms and sand. Friends of my parents, with teenaged children, camped in a circle at the end of a Fort Pickens State Park. Over many years, we blistered our skin, suffered heat stroke, had an appendix removed, menstrual cycles began and ended, oysters and paella was served for a beach dinner, stories were told and songs sung.

Dad told about "North with the Spring" while driving north to distract me from the carsickness from the raw oysters. He turned off the highway meandering on small roads of Alabama. We stopped at other-worldly gas stations with tanks of baby alligators, peacock bedspreads, and foreboding

Confederate flags. Redbuds and dogwoods flourished in the woods. The dirt was red.

After returning home, I searched at Lake Forest Library through the card files for "North with the Spring" and came across *Silent Spring*. Discovering Rachel Carson burst my world open. What mankind can do? Through rhythmic poetic writing she taught me hard science. The Bald Eagle, Great Blue Herons and Whooping Cranes were nearly extinct. If shells aren't strong enough for birds to hatch, what are chemicals doing to us? *Silent Spring* led to reading Jane Goodall and her writings of our commonality with chimpanzees. These two women emerged as my heroes. They beautifully wrote of what I yearned to learn. Of how nature connected and was changed by us. How we could change our selves for the better. Jane Goodall's *My Life with Chimpanzees* landed on Mom's pillow for her night's read. She responded with a ticket to a Jane Goodall lecture at the Auditorium theater. Our definition of being a superior intelligence is based on making tools. Jane photographed a chimpanzee making a tool. Humankind was redefined.

Easter Sunday was all about bonnets and starchy dresses, black patent leather shoes, stockings and muffs for church. Leaving the car on Illinois near Greenbay roads, Dad walked on the street side of the sidewalk, "In case a car splashed," he said. We entered the church door from the rear nearly on time. Our pew, twelve from the back, was waiting for us. It's not that it was ever assigned, the parish knew we filled the same two pews every Sunday. Most Sundays doilies or handkerchiefs were quickly bobby-pinned on the way into church. The entrance procession began with a hymn. On

Easter, bonnets flounced throughout the church. Women had veils over their faces and white gloves on their hands.

"So and so is still in mourning!" Aunt Mary Marg said seeing a woman in black with a droopy wide-brimmed hat. "Look who has a new baby!" Mom might tell Mrs. Harkens. We'd return home to an Easter hunt for eggs, chicks, jelly beans and bunnies. They represented what? Rejuvenation, rebirth, Jesus leaving the tomb, resurrection? Dying by crucifixion to resurrect to heaven? The meaning of Easter was a tough holiday to grasp.

~

Summer

June through late August days were spent on our beach. Thousands of dried, curled alewives littered the beach. Their crisped fins sliced our feet. They floated on choppy waves and piled in the thousands above the gravel. Hot sun rotted the piles of stinking flesh. House flies followed. We avoided them underwater. In July, fatty Coho Salmon lazily floated in the calm clear water, some as long as I was tall. I imagined reaching in to grab one for dinner. They were introduced to eat the alewives and stored the lake's DDT and mercury. Our soles toughened to leather running over the pebbles and sandy shore. Great flat stones captured light as they were spun to bounce in arcs on an inland sea. August brought high waves for riding into shore and migrating birds of prey.

Mom carried down a breakfast of toast and juice, eggs scrambled on a campfire and peppered with kicked sand as the sun glistened off the morning lake. She settled into her book when I first swam by stretching out my legs, walking my fingers along the sand and kicking. Silvery schools of minnows darted around my arms. The gentle waves lifted me to a float and lowered me for my fingers to touch sand. Kicking and paddling until I no longer touched down.

"Look, she's swimming!" was shouted from the Three Posts, the end of a washed away dock. My dog paddle merged to a breast-stroke with a whip kick that propelled me into the waves. My rite of passage to swim that far came with rewards of jumping. Ladder-like branches were tied for steps. Repeatedly, a wooden diving board was nailed on top of the rotting end of the dock posts. The gap with the older kids closed a bit. Practicing flips and front and back dives with our own Olympic competition scoring consumed weeks. Tying driftwood logs together with rope into rafts took hours or days. We pushed the raft, with a long green sapling, from one beach to another and dreamed of crossing Lake Michigan. Though too young, the older ones took care of the younger ones who looked after the even younger ones. Too much bossiness, too many rules invented to contain and herd what was out of control. I often felt squelchy by being reigned on by parental messages delivered from children.

Our hand impressions were pressed in recessed wet squares of sand. We added compositions of driftwood-sticks, shells and feathers weighed down with rocks. Mom mixed Plaster of Paris with lake water, and poured it into the square. She placed a metal wire in the setting plaster to hang on the stucco wall of the dining porch. Another day we might make sandcastles ringed with seaweed for gardens.

"Everyone out of the water!" Dad called down from the top the cliff, "there are seiche warnings!" We scrambled up the cliff carrying bags of towels, sand castings and water.

Later, waves broke up our raft scattering the driftwood again, ripped off our Three Posts platform, and shortened our beach into our eroding cliff. The railroad tie steps collapsed into a vertical cliff and a climbing rope was installed. We pulled our way up the steep clay steps.

~

The summer of 1966, curled up in peddle-pushers and a T-shirt on the couch reading, my hair still dripping wet from a solitary morning swim in the lake, I sat beside the bay window and wide door to the foyer. The living room was floor to ceiling books in darkly stained shelves. A fifty-gallon aquarium bubbled behind me, the huge fireplace in front not even noticed. I devoured Laura Ingalls Wilder's *Silver Lake* horrified that Mary had become blind due to a fever and wondering how she could possibly adapt to…

"Time to go!" Mom called from the bottom of the steps. I hadn't heard her high heels and I jumped up, taking my book with me. My fingers reached out the passenger window to slice down the parkway trees. No trees fell. At the highway, I cranked up the window, the no-vent windows were pulled open. An aroma of tree-lined streets and summer prairie flowers rushed in. We rode for the time it took me to finish my book. Mary did go blind and Laura described in detail everything she couldn't see. When my stomach got queasy, I pushed a fingernail through my wind-dried hair along the midline of my head and started to braid it into two tight pigtails with a rubber band at the bottom. Already, the summer sun had lightened my brunette hair.

Mom explained the Head Start program as she cruised along the four lanes laden with traffic of the Dan Ryan

Expressway. Smells of steel mills and packing houses increased my queasiness. I closed the no-vent window, glanced about for a horizon line to steady my stomach. She told me about the Southside children she taught early-childhood math and reading skills. One of her students Vanessa will stay with us for a couple weeks. My sister was away at camp and Vanessa was my age. She would stay in my room. The highway was dug under the side-streets with house high-concrete walls filled with spurting patches of yellow and blue flowering weeds. I concentrated to keep my car sick stomach behaving. A few whimpering coffee trees and broken-windowed brick buildings rose above the crawling car.

"This is the Dan Ryan Expressway. It's named after the Chairman of the Cook County Board," Mom said. Her tone told me he was like the conversations I'd heard about Cardinal Cody, but didn't understand. It was something about racially divisive actions in neighborhoods that she didn't like and that she was doing something about. We pulled off onto the side streets the wooden buildings slumped onto brick buildings. Some front gardens were seeded with flowers but not weeded. Sheets and cardboard filled in cracked and missing windows.

Young children played on front steps. Empty lots were filled with crabgrass and high with ragweed. Listless men clutching paper bags, slumped silently in front of diamond-shaped gates of closed stores. Radios blasted percussion that vibrated the windows and horns that rose to another rhythm. Liquor and Hostess snack signs were displayed in all the windows. Mom sneezed into her always-present tissue and pulled in front of several light brick tower apartments with a low-rise Head Start center. The stench of the stained streets caused my weak stomach to somersault. Earnest, coifed black mothers walked hand-in-hand with tiny daughters dressed in pink birthday party dresses above pinchy, patent-leather shoes. "For some, the dresses are all they have," Mom said.

Mom and her friends taught Vanessa, a girl my age. Quiet Vanessa, in tightly twisted pig tails with rubber bands

at the tops and tips, arrived in her Sunday best with a brown suitcase. She sat primly in the back seat of our station wagon. My worn red Keds and her black shiny dress shoes dangled diagonally from the back seat, toes pointed in. Her tightly braided stiff pigtails touched my arm. The crisp ends poked. In the hour car-ride home Vanessa was very quiet. She must have been one of my mother's favorite students. I showed her my Laura Ingalls Wilder book and told her all about Laura's

Pa who worked the horses to plow the field and milked a cow. In the evening, Pa enjoyed playing the fiddle, or a violin. Her eyes moved left to see, but her head was straight. *Mildly interested in two names for one instrument*, I told her more about his folk songs and toe tapping.

"Laura wrote about her own life in the woods and by a lake in many books," I said. Silently, she looked out the window as we sped along Edens highway. There were more and more trees as we approached the northern suburbs. A stream of tears flowed down her cheek. Mom glanced in the rear-view mirror. Two quiet girls sat side by side. My shy place in a large family had become an awkward strain of entertaining a reluctant new friend. The feeling was worse than my queasiness. By the time we drove through our front woods on a winding driveway, Vanessa appeared to be terrified. Sheba ran out of the woods barking at the car tires. Even Mom's voice couldn't calm her. Inside the courtyard, Vanessa didn't want to leave the car, so Mom left the door open and brought her suitcase inside. Later, she took her hand and cajoled her to come inside. Vanessa had not spoken a word.

~

Our Spanish-style home had seven bedrooms, three staircases, eight baths, a five-room apartment and a three-bedroom coach house wrapped around the courtyard, a garden of azaleas and a tall, old oak presiding over the entrance. Mom made sure that each of us had an art studio. Our oldest brother's darkroom was at the top of the attic steps. Hugh made his own bedroom there too, painted in black and white checkerboard to strum his guitar. A sister's loom and brother's drum set filled entire bedrooms. My wood and stone carving studio was on the back screened-porch overlooking the lake. There was music all the time. Flute scales were stacattoed behind my closed double bedroom doors. The piano room was just off the living room. Guitar, drums, harmonica, and flute scales, rocked songs with blips and mistakes up and down the hall.

Early morning hullabaloo quieted after the oldest brothers and sisters skittered down the front stairs for summer jobs. Around the corner, a closet off the mudroom with a wall of hooks for sweaters, coats, scarves above pairs of shoes where we picked a sweater or coat right for the day. I planned on wearing a pair of Redwing boots for the muddy day ahead and hoped they were still there, though they were too big. The few kids on our block of three-acre estates, and Highland Park cousins, came to our house because something was always going on.

Vanessa sat on the bottom of the grand staircase and cried. I sat to console her. Sheba whimpered and barked. Sylvia meowed. My heart ripped for Vanessa. I was hopeless at calming her so frustration set in. Vanessa watched teary-eyed from inside the bay window. In the east woods by the lake, we decided to dig a hole to China. It had to start off pretty big. Enough for four shovels to fling dirt on top of ripe "stink bombs," white fungi balls that grew as big as volley balls. "Those smell so bad!" "Hey, let's used them for nuclear bombs!!" We tossed them as high as two of us could to explode their stinking white and black powder all over the freshly mowed lawn. The whole yard and woods stunk.

We went back to digging. Over time, our hole got pretty

deep. Deep enough to let us know we were not going to get to China that summer. Thin plywood was laid over our hole and branches and leaves laid on top. We slipped into the hole and slid the mossy cover shut so nuclear bombs couldn't get us. We planned to store dried milk, more water, chocolate and beef jerky for that ominous imagined day. Dad's old Army mess kit with metal spoons and fork was set on a board, then we ran to the basement to make pottery vessels.

~

Once Dad made us wooden rubber-band guns in his basement wood shop. Carefully and slowly he carved in jointed wood, with minute detail, a replica pine .45 pistol with a wooden clothespin screwed on top. The rubber band on the barrel head was stretched to the closed-pin mouth. "Only aim at fences or trees," he said. The older boys had aimed and shot at each other before they were up the back-basement steps. Immediately, all the pistols were confiscated by Dad. "And don't chew a gun from your peanut butter sandwich either," we heard at the table. Midway through the first week, Vanessa and I felt more comfortable together. We'd grown accustom to our awkwardness with each other though I was compelled to join the *we* of my family that often left her alone.

For long days, weeks, maybe years, we played Kick-the-Can. A circle was drawn with a toe into the pea gravel in the courtyard and an empty large tin can carefully placed in the measured center. Teams from ten to twenty kids were selected and a coin tossed to decide which team held the camp or hid in the woods. Vanessa did not want to be picked first or last. She, in her pink party dress sat in a cast iron chair, once a tractor seat, on a tri-pod of legs and watched from the portico. A name was called out while the caller's foot was on the can to capture the enemy who waited in the circle. Teammates could run through the circle and kick-the-can to release all the prisoners. The game started again. Chin to knees, I hid in the courtyard yews and swatted a hovering bee's hum. The first sting and flail of my arms angered the hive. Half a dozen red welts erupted on my face and I let out an explosive holler. I ran past Vanessa's slight smile swatting a circling of bees to the kitchen.

"We will only live for four years if all the bees die," Mom consoled me while pressing copper pennies on the red blebs. Vanessa came in to silently help Mom pat my swollen and red face with a cool, wet towel. Vanessa wiped my stream of tears.

Capture the Flag consumed other days. The front woods were positioned around a central path to the tennis court, neatly dividing the dense underbrush in half. It seemed I waited forever to be picked for a team. Each team was given a red or blue bandana to hide on their side. Each team strategized to find and capture the other's flag. Cousins made up opposite teams: Stim covered Frank, Pike hovered over Andrew, Bow guarded Mary, Pat restrained Elizabeth, Peewee blocked Hugh, Noreen impeded Patrick. Underestimated little ones were tools of the schemers. I ducked down low and hid from the trunk to the trunk careful not to step on trillium. Mosquitos buzzed, webs tangled with fleeing spiders, brambles caught my tee shirt in the underbrush. Chases went on. I spotted the flag. No one noticed. Once captured, I hid it in my shirt. Skirmishes continued. The flag had to be rushed to the safe side of the woods before the capturer was tagged. I sauntered and made it to our home base. No one believed me when I called out, "Captured!" though I was standing there holding the flag.

Vanessa sat in the staircase landing window, looking out through the courtyard gate as a dozen of *us* and friends ran through the woods. I looked up to see her watching us with intent. We were called in for dinner with a large hand-rung bell from the kitchen screened porch. Vanessa sat next to me at the table where my sister, who was at camp, usually sat. She slept in my sister's bed. We bonded from being next to each other each day, girls the same age. After back porch dinners, we had enough for two softball teams. Vanessa watched from the back-brick patio framed by two screen porches as sixteen-inch softballs caught without a mitt. Batting order was usually by age. Pitching was always by the oldest boy on each team. When dusk settled to darkness, flashlight tag, ghost in the graveyard, or capturing lightning bugs filled our summer nights. We filled the bathtub to soak off the day's dirt. I read while Vanessa splashed in the tub. Her pig-tails stayed tightly braided most of the week. My pigtails were braided at least every day. Vanessa and I dozed off to sleep watching a jar of blinking lightning bugs sitting on leaves.

Mornings, we woke up together and talked quietly. Our room was at the end of the hall, more quiet as we heard feet hit the floor, water flush and shoes hit the stairs. Slowly we changed, brushed our teeth, treasuring our quiet time before the day began. She told me about her brother and sister. How they shared a room and liked to play pick-up-sticks. I told her about how Mary and I played spelling games, "Am I spelling or saying O-R-E-O?" Rainy days found us in the large attic room playing darts or with an electric train set our Gram Leahy had built a tunnel and two tracks intersecting at blinking lights that captured everyone's attention. We tried to be fair about who ran each of the two engines. Younger kids, like me, usually watched a train disappear into a tunnel, then almost collide with the other train until something broke.

Vanessa liked the attic with its six dormer windows and

slanting roof. She liked the four-square game with a rubber red ball that could be bounced so high it ricocheted off the pointed ceiling. Numbered tiny pots of paint-matched outlined numbers on a board. Instructions were included to fill in all the #7s spaces with red and #2s with yellow until an image appeared. She laughed. I relaxed. We sat in bean bag chairs and braided each other's hair.

Vanessa seemed isolated, lonely? She cried at the bottom of the steps. My cousin arrived by car to play with Vanessa. We decided we'd make some money to buy candy at the Little Store, the farthest we were allowed to walk. Rice Krispy bars were made by melting marshmallows in butter and mixing in Rice Krispy cereal, then spreading those in a buttered pan. Once it cooled, it was cut into bars and placed in a wax paper lined shoe box. Frozen lemonade concentrate was mixed, ice added. Napkins, towels and Dixie cups were packed in a brown box. Our toy cash register was found and filled with coins and single dollars. The wagon was wheeled from the shed and wiped down of spider webs. Vanessa was petrified of spider webs. With a towel on the bottom of the wagon, we carefully pulled the box of bars, Oreo cookies, and lemonade down the long driveway and to our bus stop corner on Maplewood. A car pulled up asking for Rice Krispy bars and a cup of lemonade. I turned for change from the cash register, but the money was gone! I looked at Noreen, then we looked at Vanessa. She looked away.

"Keep the change," the driver smiled.

We decided to traverse the steep eroding cliff to swim in the wonderland of the lake. Vanessa slipped on the muddy stairs. I tried to hold her hand like my sisters had held mine, but she pulled away, slipped and scrambled up. We tried drawing, television, piano. I was in pain for her and exasperated tears would begin again. Some days, nothing would subside her stream of flowing tears. Sheba barked at her tears. I barked "Quiet!" at Sheba, who barked at Vanessa. The cat was nowhere to be seen.

"Vanessa, your mother is on the phone," Mom said. Vanessa talked through her sobs. She took Mom's hand and closed the swinging butler's pantry door to talk with her mother. Mom and I silently sat in the kitchen.

"Mamma, I can't climb those stairs one more time!" Vanessa said. "I am worn out from climbing upstairs and downstairs. When I get halfway there's a window looking into dark woods that wolves run out. I can't climb one more set of stairs Mamma! Please come get me."

Mom and I drove Vanessa back to her high-rise home. She stepped out of the car, all full of bravado.

"Oh, hi, Mamma," she said nonchalantly as she gave her mother a hug then strode away. Her mother raised a brow and followed her daughter. I imagined Vanessa introducing all kinds of new games to her family and friends. She hadn't just been watching us play, she was taking notes. Vanessa chatted nonstop to her friends in the lobby.

Mom turned to me. "Would you like to stay with Vanessa's family?" This was our mothers' plan, to exchange homes and see how the other child lived. Since that question, I have wondered what it would have been like to live in an apartment in Bronzeville. Just as I was not part of the conversation to have Vanessa stay with us, I was not privy to why I didn't get to stay with her.

Vanessa's absence was bigger than her presence. I wondered, *Is Vanessa happy at home? Was she playing "Kick the Can"? Did she open a lemonade stand? Did she win at pick-up-sticks?*

In the empty feeling afterward, I tried out my brother's idle Sailfish and spent the rest of the summer learning to sail. A strong sailing wind enticed a walk along the beach to launch our sailfish at the public beach to capture the breeze. My tacking ability was honed by following the path of more experienced day sailors. I sailed as far south as Fort Sheridan's airstrip when the wind whipped off the land and as far north as Lake Bluff. Shinnok salmon and rainbow trout swam in July's clear waters. Only a few alewives shriveled on the beaches. After being caught in a thunderstorm, I learned to watch for the storm-building patterns of *cirrus* to *stratus* to *altocumulus* clouds. In high school, I taught kids to sail with the sunfish. As we got older, it led to more friends and other beaches. It had been an idyllic, sun-burning, callous-forming, constant and ever-changing paradise until it inverted.

Moldings

The summer after my eighth grade graduation, I flew to Europe with my parents and younger sister and brother for a car tour. Dad was commissioned by Continental Bank to draw banks in Milan, Paris, Brussels, Munich, Frankfort, Zurich, Lichtenstein, and London. He packed Herman Wouk's *Winds of War*. We traveled as a professor's family with Youth Hostel cards and slept where we landed each night, sometimes using camping gear with no reservations anywhere. Dad and Mom wanted to show us Europe. Their older kids had the Spain experience.

"We're going to crash!" I woke up shaking Jean. "The plane has stopped!" Northern Lights danced on the tips of our wings convincing me that the plane had frozen in mid-flight. My sister calmed me with hushed whispers. Sleepy, disturbed passengers barely looked out the windows. *Did I somehow remember my infant flight with the failed engine?* We landed in Milan and shopped at the Galleria before visiting Dad who perched on his wobbly camp chair on the sidewalk, hunkered over a drawing with throngs of onlookers who watched each line become a representational, then cubistic interpretation of the city scene before us. "I draw what happens over time," Dad said to the spectators, "and what is around the corner. It is a timeline of one day." When Dad wasn't drawing, or driving our tiny Fiat, he was reading Wouk's reminiscence of WWII. We revisited his war experience from Wouk's perspective. Dad didn't like to camp at home, but we camped in Europe. Already six feet tall, the gangly three of us shared the Fiat back seat, squished while rounding the switchbacks in the French and Swiss Alps.

In Switzerland, I awoke at dawn to hike a cow path up to a tiny, icy, and clear turquoise mountain lake for a morning skinny-dip in melted snow. A few birds offered melody to clanking cow bells that gave rhythm to the red glow of a dawning day. As the sun warmed above the mountain peaks, I retraced the path down, greeted by a stream of hikers speaking dozens of languages: "Good Morning." *Suisserduetch* "*Buongiorno.*" I'd repeat "*Boungiorno*" to the next person who would reply in Spanish "*Buenos Dias.*" I greeted the next German hiker with the Spanish version, then German to an Italian and so on for tens of languages and hikers. At thirteen, I was horrified to think of how many would have seen me swimming if I hadn't dressed even moments later.

~

"Don't use the water to brush your teeth!" Mom said. On our way to Belgium, we stopped in traffic. One European driver got out of his car to talk in German to a driver, then

French to another in the next car, then Spanish to a third. When he got to our car he lifted his hands and enunciated in clear American English, "They're all Sunday Drivers." I realized how isolated the Midwest is from the rest of the world and, even more so, Lake Forest from the Midwest. When we visited the Calais beaches Dad read from Wouk's book while a horse cantered along the surf at sunset. Churchill had to decide to allow a camp of Allied forces to be bombed for a large number of England's army to have the chance to cross the channel to England. Private boats picked up the soldiers from the beach to transport them to England as military ships were bombed. Dad wanted to camp here, Mom wasn't sure it was safe. We found a hotel room. I was still vegetarian at the time and grasped enough language to request pasta *parmesan solemente* or *sans boeuf.* French waitresses were very concerned. "You must eat meat!" they said.

We stopped at each little French town for a loaf of fresh bread or *pomme frittes* that held me over. We drove into Paris late at night with no hotel reservations during Bastille Day weekend. Every hotel was full. Very late, we all got out of the car to knock on a door in a sketchy block of Paris. An elder woman with half her head black and the other white opened the top half of the door, "*Bonswaana!*" she greeted us. *Haunted* I thought, but nodded when Dad asked me for an okay. The pull cord loo was on a landing shared by two floors. When I opened the French doors to our railed porch in the morn, a naked man stood across the street singing from his balcony. I quickly shut doors to keep my younger brother and sister from seeing.

"Remember, don't use tap water to brush your teeth,"

Mom said. I walked along a bank of the Seine and into a pet shop that had squirrel monkeys and parrots, squirrels and minks. Dad and I visited his favorite art stores in Paris, Berlin and London where he replenished his preferred 100 pound Arches paper and veri-black pencils. One day in Paris, my mother and I searched until we found Auguste Rodin's Museum where I felt the spirit of individual men through their sculpted bronze faces. I saw Rodin's bronze-cast eyes expose the souls of men who lived a hundred years ago. I felt the vitality and mentioned to my mother that I would like to try that at home. We drove out of Paris.

~

One month in historic Europe made me aware of the gift of fresh water and a desire to sculpt. At fourteen, I started finding people's faces in clay. Sylvia Shaw Judson, who sculpted *The Bird Girl*, came to dinner and politely viewed my first attempts. She invited me to work with her on Saturdays in her Ragdale studio. Sylvia sculpted small and quiet things made powerful in form. She taught me that the visible form expresses the spirit within. She taught me how to testify to the enormous importance of life forms while showing me how to build an armature for clay, make a mold, and cast it in bronze. Sylvia showed me a woman could be a sculptor as well as a mother. With my driver's license, Mom arranged for me to take Tuesday mornings off school to sculpt with the internationally-known artist Abbott Pattison who taught me carving, constructing, and modeling techniques. Sculpture burst open with new skills to make representational and abstract art.

Over three summers, Pat and I, with friends, canoed in

the Quetico. With Duluth packs on our backs and canoes on our shoulders, we portaged from rock to rock, poured salt on the leeches and started our life-long birdwatching. We dragged a fish line for cooking our dinners, charted courses to stashes of jellies and often slept in the canoes and witnessed one of the most remarkable Northern Light displays of our lifetime. Multicolored dancing lights filled the sky on a night without mosquitos. I learned later the light shows were caused by explosions on the sun. We slept in the open, exhausted from a full day of traversing lakes and portages.

~

"Bless us oh Lord and these thy gifts that we are about to receive..." the churning repetitive hum of summer cicadas raised our decibel level. We were sitting on the back porch at dinner, each of us before the folded napkin on the left then the fork, a plate and knives and spoon on the right with a glass above those. Freshly cut zinnias were in a low vase in the center. The sand castings blended into the stucco wall. I positioned myself to overlook the lake. The complexity played itself out in a discussion of who got the car that night. Sheba leapt at a morsel of dropped food. The phone rang.

Pat called, "Do you want a horse?" She was given two to care for by her neighbor.

"*Yes!*" I answered, not believing the moment. We had talked about getting horses for years, shared our birthday week through grade school, bird watched and canoed together. Mom noticed my excitement. Pat and I would ride horses together. I couldn't believe it was true! Pat's friend had gone to college and the family wanted to keep the horses in the barn and field. And so my high school years included taming a wild Duchess to not run at full speed into the barn, to jump low fences in the pasture and race and race through corn fields. Pat, with Nugget, and I, with Duchess, trotted through West Lake Forest's fields and woods.

Along the western edge of Lake Forest, we rode our horses to McCormick's Pond, slipped off the saddles and swam on horses bareback. They shot off their last foot hold to dog paddle at a trot speed. We strapped sleeping bags on back of the saddle with saddle bags filled with food and grain and camped overnight. One Thanksgiving, my cousin and I rode ten miles to Lake Michigan, then back after dinner. For Halloween, we buttoned raincoats over our heads, carried jack lanterns and rode around the streets surprising trick-or-treaters as the headless horsemen. In the winter, we'd harness one horse and she'd ski behind, while I rode bareback. West Lake Forest's prairies were a completely new environment from the lakefront forests. I worked Saturdays at Lake Forest Bookstore, babysitting and as a lifeguard to earn money for vets, oats and hay.

Robin, a biology classmate, explained *virgin prairies* had *native plants:* crown vetch, spurge, burdock, fleabane and spiderwort in biology class. Some plants still sounded like weeds. With a heightened awareness; cinquefoil, shooting star, turks cap, lupine, Jo Pie and butter and eggs emerged as we appreciated the root and seed producing systems of prairie plants. Red Winged Black birds and bluebirds flitted their colors in the glistening dew of the turkey foot grasses. Great Blue Herons and Whooping Cranes were endangered. Robin controlled burning the prairies to reduce invasive species and release seeds by heat. From the priory in Lake Bluff, he and I walked the creek path behind Ragdale and into their prairie. We discovered the artesian well in the middle. He was excited that Ragdale's prairie was possibly a virgin prairie that had never been farmed. Robin, with a naturalist, came to see me at the Lake Forest Bookstore. They wanted an introduction to Sylvia Shaw Haskins. After that meeting, she and her daughter Alice Hayes gave the back fifty acres of virgin prairie on Greenbay Road to the Nature Conservancy—now cared for by Open Lands. The mother and daughter decided to open an artist retreat with the front four acres, Ragdale house and red barn.

~

That summer my mother asked, "Would you like to live with Gram in a Lake Forest apartment during my senior year?" Her hardwood carved furniture, depression glass and china were moved from California to an apartment above Deerpath theater. Gramma Mac and I ate bacon, liver and caramelized onions for breakfast, lunch and dinner. I spent our time asking questions about her family and Dad's childhood while she envisioned deceased Jack passing by her furniture and through the apartment. I never met any of my great aunts or uncles, but she was from a large family.

"Margot, just look forward." Gram would say. Or a thought-provoking phrase, "my parents were bedridden. Eva and I were busy working to feed the children who were on their own. I hope you will never know the difficulties in the life I have known." *How could I not keep asking questions?*

"There is a place near Ausable Forks," she began. "It's near Lake George. Lake George is grand! I was married near

Ausable Forks in a church. I wanted my savings for furniture not a big wedding," she trailed off into memory. She'd point to an ad in a magazine, "See how beautiful her neckline is…I always wanted to be an artist."

My cousin Noreen and I couldn't find Gramma Mac in her apartment after school one day. I called Dad. He searched by car. Noreen and I scoured the town. Gram was found getting off the Chicago Northwestern train after "visiting friends in the city." That evening she had a massive stroke. I moved back home to Airdrie and visited Gram in the hospital. One late afternoon, while the shadows were long and just before the darting swifts were replaced by swooping bats, Gram passed away. At her wake, I met a lifetime of family, friends, work associates outside of Gram's Sunday visits. I knew nothing of her work life or siblings.

"She was a remarkable woman," a gentleman paused to tell me. "Always looked out for others and felt her way clearly through life. Very classy." I wanted to know more. I drove fast on Westleigh Road to West Campus classes with the car still bouncing a bit from going over the bridge. I hit a low point of missing her, my independence of us watching out for each other, and loss of living in an apartment in town. Frustrated with my questions she deflected masterfully, "It was all grand!" My grief settled in and I pulled over. I felt her say out loud, "I have no hunger, no thirst, no want or need. I don't have pain or sorrow. Don't be sad for me because I'm myself now without burdens. If you are sad it is for yourself, not for me." I didn't feel sorrow for her passing again.

With Dad ensuring we were educated before college, I heard Buckminster Fuller explain comprehensive design science of artifacts like the geodesic dome for sustainable living, John Cage's music from everyday staccatos of sounds and silence. Both influenced my audio taping the Springtime Cardinal, Robin and Chickadee songs to arrange into Hayden's Spring Sonata Allegra patterns for a music composition assignment. I had the sand of Lake Michigan and the soil of the prairies still in my shoe laces. My Fry boots were worn by ravines in search of birds and along beaches collecting driftwood. My skin was darkened, hair lightened from the reflection of the sun from sailing Lake Michigan waves. My back was challenged by bareback horse rides through the forests, lakes, and prairies. I wasn't the same as the previous six brothers and sisters. I didn't transplant well. I won't grow straight with trimmed, transplanted roots. I tried, but had too much broad rooted, webbed inter-connection here. Friends flourished in various circles, connected by sports, ecology, literature or art. I learned to sculpt here. To reach my full height, as an artist, I needed to draw strength from my tap root. I will come home again. I packed my bags for college.

~

7am: Garrison Keillor radio show; 8am: Renaissance Art History; 10 am: Biology; 1pm: Drawing I on Monday, Wednesday and Friday. 9am: American Renaissance Literature; 11am: French; 1-4pm: Sculpture on Tuesdays and Thursdays; 4pm: violin Thursday; 12pm: bagpipes 12pm Friday. Homework until midnight. I'd landed at Hamline University with a full line-up of classes in a consortium.

Thumbprints mashed into wet clay, delineating differences. I sculpted one head with a raw honesty of my search for a likeness. Knives cutting the surface, scraping the form for my imagined image until the head was proportionately unique. Twice a week, for hours and months I pushed and sliced clay, then threw wet plaster at it to harden, making a thick shell mold in two parts. Both mold halves were broken away with prying metal rods. Burning hot wax was poured into the fragile interior of that shell with fine fins from etched lines, rolled around, poured out, then repeated. That wax image was seared with a white soldering wire to attach vertical tubular sprues that were fused to a cup. Hot metal pins poked through the thin skin to hold placement in the mold. Months of clay sculpting was placed in a metal cylinder. Vermiculite, sand and plaster was poured inside and around the wax shell and left to set until rock hard. When inverted into a kiln, a gas flame burned overnight to harden the mold and leave a lost wax space. I tended the burning kiln and lifted the mold's hotness with foundry gloves into a sand pit that steadied the pouring of sputtering splashes of molten bronze into the empty space. Surprisingly, transforming pliable clay into solid metal was seeing my sculpture for the first time. With a liver sulfate and iron oxide patina, I gave my first bronze portrait to Mom and Dad for Christmas.

What caused Dad and I to argue over a mere chickadee at the kitchen window feeder, I'll never know. We were sitting at Airdrie's, having toast and marmalade at the kitchen table. He had a cup of coffee. I silently drank a vitamin concoction blended with beets that gave me three hours of energy to finish my extended class-work. Mom quietly hovered, used to the transitions from college, apartments, and visits with spouses. "You never come home again," he quoted some great author from *The New Yorker* on the table. We were at odds for many reasons and he wanted to remind me I hadn't been tested by life yet. In response to my new confidence from my sculpture and studies, Dad read a cartoon, "Pointy heads that can't park a bicycle straight." Though my pre-med track was woefully compromised, I'd come home after being hospitalized with hepatitis in college. They were concerned.

"Don't forget to do the dishes." Dad saw the confidence I'd come home from college with and wanted to remind me of a woman's role in life. I chafed at his demeaning ancient ways. *How does that advice match his liberal point of view?* "Wear stockings and a dress to your interviews," he told me. *Not anymore, she would only take a job where pants were allowed—blue jeans preferable.* Mom rolled her eyes at the opportunities I was snubbing. "If you can type you can get a job anywhere," Mom said.

"Would you look at that chickadee!" Dad pointed to the black, hooded, gray bird upside down at the birdfeeder.

"That's not a chickadee!" I surprised myself with how the words exploded with confidence.

"That is a chickadee," he said and stepped out of the room.

...or nuthatch, I thought. The silences of their arguments were louder than a bomb. We'd been negotiating my preparations for a summertime mountain-climbing trip with new college friends. Three days a week I'd jogged through St. Paul's snowy sidewalks to get in shape with friends. We rock climbed on Saturdays at Taylor's Falls and ice climbed once or twice at the Mushroom Caves while I swam one hundred laps a week. My parents considered climbing a waste of time. My belay lines, carabiners, crampons and ice pick were

purchased from my summer landscaping job. My parents didn't engage in more conversation, sure climbing would blow over, pretty sure their "fragile little flower" as my father called me, would come to my senses. I was too tired to care.

~

I knew I needed to get some fresh air, move. I needed to get out of bed. I had to get going! I had to get out of this malaise.

A few days later, the cold January sun came out. Inspired by my uncle's story, I attempted climbing down the backyard cliff I'd easily traversed since preschool. I could barely balance, and squatted with vertigo. I reversed down the steep incline on all fours. The walk along the beach didn't last long. I climbed up clinging with my fingertips and toes. *Tomorrow I will try again.* A week of walks and eating regularly helped. I packed my clothes for school, and would recover.

~

Well enough to return to college in February, I studied the course lists. Asian Literature and Micronesia Art History jumped off the page. The repetitions of schedule set in: Garrison Keillor, Art History, Comparative Biology II, Drawing II, Literature, Sculpture II, Fencing. Homework until midnight. In spring, I joined the tennis team to get back in shape. We practiced with down jackets on outdoor courts with dirty, drifted snow along a cyclone fence. Clumps of snow clung to the diamond patterns and fell to explode into crystals if jolted by a wayward slow bouncing ball. Matches were played in Duluth, Mankato, and Rochester. My partner and I laughed so hard at mistakes we'd fall on the court.

In literature, I'd read about folk characters, a monkey

spirit traveling between earth and heaven with wisdom and mischievous antics. India's Hindu deity Gnesh, with multiple arms. The five-thousand-year old Sepik River culture honored crocodiles that grew to twenty-five feet long, with jaws as long as a person. I learned Hooli lived in the mountains and prized the family's pig. The boys grew eighteen inches of hair, had it ceremoniously cut and woven into a wig. Paint was carefully applied to the wigmen in spirit houses. The Fresh Sepik River was the largest body of fresh water in Micronesia. Eight hundred and thirty-two New Guinea languages, including sign, kept clan secrets and made New Guinee the most linguistically diverse place on earth. I learned the locations of New Guinea, the Philippines, their proximity to Japan, China and India. For my final report, I carved a Sepik River fertility symbol in mahogany while imagining myself being a Hooli artisan. In sculpture class, I made in clay and cast in bronze a full figure. Their drawing model actually had six toes!

~

"Only take calculated risks," Mom said. Turned out, she and Jean came to convince me not to climb mountains. Mom drove to my Wisconsin camp where I taught sailing for the summer and hoped to take me home.

"I've worked hard for this all year," I said. "I bought all the equipment." It was 1976 and I wanted adventure.

"Why don't you let it go?" my mother said.

"Because I can," I said. "I want to do this, Mom." My family didn't drive through to view mountains. They experienced, witnessed and documented travels. I promised to journal, to photograph and draw. After all, my mother had climbed into sputtering propeller airplanes at my age. She may have quarreled similarly with her mother.

"That was for a greater purpose," my Mom argued. Mom reluctantly agreed to let me go. "As long as your sister joins you," she said. *Why did I feel the need to climb mountains?*

A week later, my sister Jean, a friend, Mike, his friends and I packed our equipment to climb the Bugaboos of the Purnell range in British Columbia and Athabasca by the Columbia Ice field in Jasper Park, Alberta, Canada. Caravanning in a Beetle we named *Athabasca*, we push-started across the country. The car's starter quit in the Dakotas. I grew nervous about my sister's safety. *How could I have endangered her?* My sister's frustration with my company in a caravan of young men driving to the mountains to bike and climb was valid. We stayed in Golden overnight and provisioned with Rosehip tea, dried beef, eggs and rye bread. I was shut down with a barrage of emotions knowing I was responsible for Jean. *What had I gotten us into?* The expansive, snow-capped grandeur of the Canadian Rockies were awe inspiring! After wrapping our car tires with chicken wire to ward off porcupines, we ascended rocky traversing paths with fragile, brightly colored flowers emerging from the fresh snow, finally reaching the tree-lined beginnings of glaciers in the Purnell range. "There's my fragile flower," was how my father had often greeted me.

We trudged with heavy packs upward and raised tents in a great snow that fell day and night. Waiting for the weather to clear, we played cards for three days. Low, distant rumbles alerted us to poke our heads through the unzipped tent to watch the collapsing avalanches explode down valley chutes of the enormous, sheering, calving glaciers. Here in the tent was fine by me. A rainy day below our tree-line was a blizzard above on Crescent Glacier. After days of reading, playing hearts and visiting the domed huts at Boulder camp, we set out. Our glacier goggles shielded our eyes from clear skies and blinding snow. Crampons were essential. Ice picks were also, as we were about to find out.

Five climbers traversed the Bugaboo Mountain glacial field, roped together because of snow-covered crevasses. On top of Bugaboo, they traversed an open field of ice. Suddenly, their leader, Mike, slipped into a crevasse that curved under so fast he seemed to disappear in front of us. *Act now! Minimize danger! Stay calm. Decide on a solution.* The more he struggled the deeper he slipped under.

"Just stop!" I called. "Don't struggle against the ice. Stay still!" Mike dug in his pick and hung on. Panic set in with the climbers. Mike was our leader. I had to act fast. Second in line, I pulled my line taut to hold him, clung to a grounded pick while lying prone, crampon toes dug deep in the snow. After a moment's pause, a plan emerged. We chocked, or fit a trapezoid with a loop, into a rock for the next climber of the chain to belay, with my line taut. The loop held fast on a chock in the fissure that allowed a carabiner clipped to it and the belayer's waist harness to stabilize the climber to the rock. The belay line end was held tight across the climber's pelvis. The rope was released or shortened by holding both ends around the belayer's hip.

The fourth climber came around to pull Mike out, while the third belayed the rescuer. All four climbers remained linked by lines. Slithering forward, I tightened Mike's line, replanting my pick, as he was pulled out, thankfully with no sprains or breaks. I worried whether Mike's limbs were intact, and if he could continue climbing. What would Voytek Kurtik, pioneer of alpine climbing, do? Our adrenaline was spent, but we managed to restore Mike's energy with oatmeal snacks and resumed ascending one of the twin peaks. My sheer exaltation of having extracted Mike from the curved fissure was inspiring. The views from the summit were gorgeous beyond belief. On the summit, we celebrated by adding stones to the cairn, empowering us with climbers before and after our ascent. The things humans could do!

Climbing Mount Athabasca was trickier. We started before dawn, consistently roped together alpine style, we each carried backpacks of crampons, chocks, carabiners, picks, helmets, water and snacks enough for a one-day climb. The traverse under the rise was a wonderland of ice bridges and drifted snow canyons. Of the five of us who began the deep glistening snow hike to the face, only Mike and I continued past the first ice bridge to the base of Athabasca. There was no way I was coming this far and not cross that bridge! Thank God we accepted their food and water! I guess we were headed for a light day of alpine climbing, Voytek Kurtik style. Voytek and his friend could climb Polish mountains like no one else! Obsessive, meticulous, precision made him the best. *Time to channel Voytek.*

Our metal teeth of the crampons strapped onto hiking boot soles bit into the crystal-clear twenty-foot long ice bridge. I roped around a rock and belayed Mike as he crossed with pick in hand. The arching bridge didn't break! I was belayed from the other side. With disbelief, I cautiously stepped on crampon tips over a two-foot-wide blue ice bridge that was likely thirty feet above fluffy white snow. *If I can cross that, I can do anything.* Knee-deep in fluffy snow, we arrived at the Athabasca's face. Snow shoes would have been helpful. The sheer cliff rose to the left of the active and moving Columbia Icefield.

~

Two, eight, twenty rope lengths, we repeatedly belayed one climber from above, while the other ascended by tenaciously ice pick pulling up the sheer face. My crampon tips kicked into slick, white ice, like ladder climbing, as I chopped the pick tip above and into ice to pull myself up. I reached Mike's belay spot, then climbed a rope's length above him. I set a belay and he climbed the length up to, then beyond me. Often, a chock was wedged too firmly in the crack and left behind. The deceptive mountain face had a sloping, rounded, vertical wall. Each of our rope lengths looked like the last belay one to the summit. Methodically, Mike and I ascended, but how would we get down? This climb is too sheer to back down.

"Should we keep going or head back?" We discussed at each passing of the belay line.

"There is no way I'm going down that sheer face! How much farther?" Mike said.

"It should only be a few more rope lengths to the top?" I said. "Let's go!" My energy increased with the adrenaline, the beauty. I recognized myself on this sheer rock face. *I'm supposed to be here.* The thick white snow was far below us as we ascended the icy, bowed rock face. At first it didn't seem very far to the top. I was fooled over and over again by the bowed perspective. At the far end of the valley, we pointed and waved as tour buses stopped for viewers to add a quarter to the binoculars and watch our ascent. Tourists could see how far we had to go. Every twenty rope lengths, I nibbled on a power bar, gaining energy from the magnificent snowy peak under a summer sun. Beauty was a communication with a higher world. The views made our strenuous effort worth it. Already we rationed water. Eight, ten rope-lengths higher. The summit lured us, teased us. No other climbers were on this face. We had a guide book and our will.

Voytek had invented a word, *CREA*. It was mental oxygen, friendship. *CREA* was about creativity being more important than creation. As long as *CREA* functioned within us, we're alive. I could feel on this climb what *CREA* was. *CREA* was energy from the surrounding beauty and dependence on another. They were constantly just two rope-lengths from the top ridge all afternoon. It was like a bad dream when you can't reach where you are going. Fear-fueled adrenaline kept us going. Hours of endurance wore us out. *Why was I here?*

At sunset, we reached the razor-edged crest with wind whisking up from a several-mile-deep back side. *I feel made to climb mountains—who knew?* Any cairn of rocks, piled to recognize the peak of Athabasca, was buried in drifted snow. Bright white snow blew powerfully from both sides of the thin ridge into red reflections of a waning sun. We dared not take a break. Hiking just below the wind's edge at dusk, we traversed drifted snow to the scree-sloped side of the face, not daring to descend what we had just ascended. Twelve hours of climbing, with mere nibbles and sips of water from day packs, and now we couldn't keep the icy wind from whipping through our clothing. I added snow to replenish my water bottle. *I am at home on this wind-blown ridge. From the flat Midwest, how is this familiar?* Ahead, the Columbia Icefield was a slow river of frozen ice. The expanse of miles of fresh white snow stretched to the horizons with a setting golden sun and rose dusk. *CREA; I climb for the connection to nature and the beauty.*

"We're not going to find Tom Crean here!" Mike joked in a shout. "Wouldn't a herd of long horn antelope look nice along that expanse of ice." Tom Crean was an Kerryman who joined Captain Scott to be one of the first to reach the South Pole. His remarkable personality, calmness, courage and endurance saved many adventurer's lives during years of traversing the Antarctic.

"Good idea to channel Tom Crean now. Voytek got us up the mountain, Crean's courage will get us down," I said. "It has got to be easier to crisscross a glacier." A nearly full moon reflected off the snow with a bright glow. Our humor kept me calm. "Let's keep descending by moonlight," Mike said. *They must be wondering about us at camp? We ARE going to make it back safely! It's like I've lived this before.*

A food and water break caused hunger. Exhaustion and delirium set in under a full moon reflecting off drifting snow. Mike and I descending a scree-path just as darkness set in. The wind calmed. Fatigue ruled. Though our adrenalin was high, we chose to chock to a crack in the cliff above a leveled scree-ledge to rest until dawn. We ate most of our chocolate with dried fruit and rye crackers. Rationed food would fuel our tomorrow. *This tethering to the side of a mountain is also familiar.* I had learned from sculpting that safety came first.

Tools and protection allows more to be done preserving effort. That training was easy to adapt to climbing. Because of the cold, we took turns, sleeping and waking the other every twenty minutes to jog in place and warm the extremities. Water from snow was not an issue. It melted inside our coats. *Stomp your feet. Wiggle your toes!* Thawing my fingers took time. My toes no longer warmed up. While rummaging Mike's pack for food, I pulled out two fist-grips with alligator jaws.

"What are these for?" I said.

"You slip this side of the juniper onto your rope and when you pull down the grip tightens." Mike said. I tried the juniper. Haphazardly, one juniper was put into my pack. Most of our conversation was planning how to get through a narrow chute with only one chock left. We needed two. Even with this broken few hours of sleep, we greeted dawn rested, concerned, and ready. The expansive warming sun shone over the colossal glacier. Its rise encouraged our descent along its edge. Scree gave way to a steep cliff. Slowly and carefully we wound our way across the glacier of snow and crevasses sometimes backtracking if the cracks were impenetrably webbed. When no rocks were available, one of us would go forward and lie prone with crampons and ice pick dug in for the other to advance. Progress was slow and tedious. I could no longer feel the cold in my legs and arms. I was hours beyond hunger. Only careful, cautious forward motion mattered. *I have the endurance and drive to be a good climber.* Horizontal and treacherous crossing of the deceptive glacier tested their nerves.

"What would Tom Crean do?" I asked.

"Probably go unleashed—forget it," Mike said.

In the lead, I came to a light, fluffy area in the snow along the scree bank. Not so different from other fissures in the glacier surface but we had reached a dead end in the maze between crevasses. I signaled back that the snow looked airy, then poked at the spot with my pick. I hammered the spot harder. Mike dug in with his pick. I sat down and kicked it with two heels, then signaled back. Cautiously, carefully, I stomped on the light snow. I signaled back that I was going ahead and Mike nodded. I took another step. Silence.

~

No sun, no wind. Kaleidoscopic, effervescent rainbows of every shade of purple, red, yellow and orange vibrated in midair and unfathomably deep into blueish tones, blurring vapor and reflections in solid ice. I was mesmerized with wonder. Perplexing dancing pigment floated below, above, and around me. The air was vibrating with bright white falling flurries. Deep in the ice colors sparkled, green, gold, then red, dancing in swirls. *Alice in Wonderland*. This was beyond what I had ever imagined. Vibrancy and prisms, endless depths of dancing color. Overwhelmed by an intense beauty my mind transcended tangible thought. An unrecognizable world swirled around me.

"Margot!" Mike called. Where was he? Above? I looked up through two slick, widening, clear, blue-ice walls. My ice pick dangled several feet above my reach. A broken hole above that and sunlight streamed down spotlighting floating snowflakes. My crampons tips were stuck with a tip-toe hold on either side of a steep vertical chasm that narrowed hundreds of feet below me. Rainbows of bright rose, glistening gold, animated blue and energetic green. I was surrounded by pure beauty, the walls vibrated with hues. Disoriented, I heard "Margot!" being called from above the hole that was up twenty-feet from where I had fallen through. *This is a crevasse.*

"I've tied your line around a rock," Mike said. "Come straight up the hole you entered. I'll belay you up. Take it easy!" Mike's even calmer than usual voice caused me to be concerned. This hole of ice was like a beautiful dream that I didn't want to leave, but I need to get out. Reality sank in. "I'm in a crevasse! A person lives fifteen minutes before hypothermia sets in." I started to think fast. The juniper! I fished the hand grip out of the top of my back pack. Without losing the toe-hold of my metal points in ice, I slipped it on the taut line and pulled myself up to my ice pick. With two crampon-tip holds, the ice pick and sliding the juniper up the rope, the climb out was possible. As the rope slackened, Mike set up a belay to keep my line taut. A sloping shelf gave me a place to dig crampons into a surface. I started to climb across an ice bulge into a bright spot in the snow and broke through the snow above with my pick. I climbed out a freshly opened hole and sheepishly said. "I know, I'm not supposed to exit another hole, but I'm out."

"Not to worry, grab onto a rock." Mike was even more composed. I was concerned.

"Untie your line, I'll pull it through the holes. I'm still chocked to the rock," he called out. I clipped my carabiner to a chock in a wall crevice, dropped my line through the hole. Mike coiled the line and tossed it to me above the openings. When I was clipped on belay I began to move from the rock.

I wondered if he'd gotten hurt while stopping my fall? *He was awfully quiet. He must have been dragged as he slowed my fall a rope length.*

"Thanks for slowing my fall so I could gracefully land a toe hold," I said.

"I got scraped up while being dragged." Mike said, "But, I'm good enough to go."

Miles below, we waved to what looked like Jean and their friends along the moraines at the bottom. *They must be a mile away.* Jean and the other dots paused and pointed up, and started to run to the base of the glacier. Busses emptied tourists at the "pay to look" binoculars again. *The joy of seeing Jean! Stay calm. Relief. Keep your wits about you!* They waved back.

A tough decision lay ahead. We could go around a rock wall which would take a few more hours or slip through a narrow gap between to two rock outcroppings and be down in an hour. There was a stretch just below the passageway where one of us couldn't be chocked on for the second belay, because we had only one more chock and needed it on top and below this gap. If Mike could take out the top chock, we'd have it for the lower levels. I would descend on belay through the gap, brace against a rock and belay him to where he can move the chock. With our fatigue and exhausted food, we chose the shorter route.

"If we make this, I'm going to nominate you for an American Alpine Climbing Award?"

"After we make this I'm going to give my crampons to…?" I said. Humor helped us to swallow the fear, kept our muscles from twitching.

Mike could stop quicker if he slipped, so I went first. Our guidebook said to head to a wall on the left of the narrow chute to a fissure for a chock. I was learning the power of will and what humans could endure. I learned I could transcend my fear for a greater gain. I learned the importance of belief. Believe you can do this and it will happen.

"Be careful," Mike said using our last chock to belay my advance through the narrow gap to as far as our line would extend to the left. The snow was deep. Tensions escalated. I needed to make each step a careful one as I crossed the chute of deep snow. Total concentration mattered. This was the real deal. Knowing my sister was headed to the base of the mountain pinpointed my concentration. *Act carefully.* I advanced to the outcrop on the left with trepidation. *In me is the answer to why I climb. I am good at this.*

"I found a chock another climber left!" I locked my carabiner on a chock and called back.

Safely, Mike was belayed through the gap and down a length of deep snow. He used the last chock again on a rock to belay me down two lengths. Within several line-lengths we were off the face and on level ground. We could unleash and run down the cascaded snow. Jean and a few friends ran to greet us at the bottom of the deep snow chute. We scarfed down peanut butter sandwiches and chugged Gatorade. Hugs of relief calmed the anxiety they hadn't allowed to surface. Stories in babbles of moments without a coherent story line flowed. It was mid-day over the Columbia Icefield.

The next morning, we cut the chicken wire off the VW Beetle's tires and headed east to Minneapolis, push-starting at every stop. Mike and I assembled a slideshow with a script, drawings and photographs. Jean, Mom and Dad, and Mike, and his parents gathered at Airdrie's dark living room to see our narrated show. Mom had not grasped the harrowing moments until the story was projected. *Maybe it was better Mom didn't know?* With my parents' unified love of cutting-edge flight and travel, a part of them understood. A part of them would have done the same thing. That was the way it was.

Set in Stone

Sophomore year, I entered the William Kugler Musical Instrument Museum for advice as to why my clay flute lost its tone after being bisque fired. For the rest of my college years I popped into this museum to help with the school tours. From tall walls of instruments on wheels, we handed ostrich egg sitars and black sea comenches to small children to strum. One wall were examples of the centuries-old progression of string instruments that lead up to making violins, starting with the black sea comenche. It was his nickelodeon collection the Smithsonian was intrigued with. Those lined the walls covered in tarps.

January term of 1977, my cousin Sheila and I traveled to Ireland to visit relatives on her mother's side. We earned independent study credits for Irish music from an Anthropology of words for her and Art History of Musical Instruments for my course. Her Aunt Letitia Gorby in Bray was our base camp. We traveled by train from Dublin along the North Sea during a fierce storm. We repeated: 1 Martello Terrace, Strand Road, Bray. The Bray station was across from Strand Road and a park to Aunt Letitia's home. 1 Martello Terrace, Strand Road. With our backpacks on, Sheila and I linked arms and stepped into the ferocious wind across Strand Road. One foot forward and two blown back we inched across the park in what seemed like an hour. Unrelenting wind and driving horizontal rain forcefully pushed us from our next gliding step: 1 Martello Terrace. If we raised a foot we'd lose our balance. *Is 1 Martello Terrace the left side or right side of the row at the end of the green?* Our eyes watered, our mouths zipped from the cold rain, our soaked heads down. The diagonal traverse ended at the last door right on the sea.

"You look like drowned field mice," was Aunt Letitia's greeting. "I've been watching you since you started across that blimey park. What a sight the two of you are. I wasn't sure you'd make it until tomorrow." We sat after changing our drenched clothes for a pot of black tea and biscuits. Her stories started when we entered with nary a pause as she fluidly covered family, Irish life, her connection with Aunt Mary Margaret and gratitude to Uncle Harry with amazing details that I'd wish I'd recorded in her lovely and lively brogue. The waves of the sea continued to pound in the side of her jolted three story house. I settled into the soft winged living room chair worn from the jet lag travel and weather. I thought I'd never rise again. She jumped up to fetch a book.

"You're an artist I've heard. Come here and sit in the dining room. Now look out that window." I glanced back over the park with rain plummeting diagonally in sheets on the soaked green. The wind roared.

"Here, read the first paragraph." The cover of the book was James Joyce's *Portrait of an Artist as a Young Man*. I read the first page.

"He wrote those words about sitting right here in this house looking out that window." She started with the full impact of Irish literature history and storytelling. Sheila and

I learned everything we could about Irish storytelling. We heard the Gorby stories of relatives from Cavan to Dublin, Bray and Monkstown. She'd arranged for us to visit an Australian uilean pipe maker in Monkstown as soon as we'd dried our things. A Gorby would host us there. As her quick and lively heavy brogue triggered story after story, our heads began to nod beyond what strong tea could revive. Quick as a rabbit she leapt up to the whistle of the tea pot on the peat burning stove to fill our red water bottles to heat the beds. We climbed her staircase to the second floor with the rain dripping from the clerestory. Buckets and rags helped.

Our huge double bed had four posts with curtains to contain our warmth. The rubber water bottles were tucked in for our toes. "No need to use the wash basins, the bathroom is down the hall," she cheerily guided. "Now find you pajamas and brush your teeth before bed. I'm delighted with your visit. Good night girls." Uncle Harry had provided for Aunt Letitia through the troubles in Ireland when she was widowed and struggling to make ends meet. Her daughter Astrid had hosted us in Wales where she lived in an abandoned chapel with a basement carved out of chalk and was married to a deer manager for an extensive estate. Every meal was venison: curried, stewed, ground for burgers. Her son Ambrose, a delivery man, would pick us up in several days to see the family's home in Cavan County. We were asleep before our heads hit the pillow.

I heard Aunt Letitia up before dawn. Sheila and I laugh at our toes reaching just over five feet of person next to six feet of person. We rose to help as the storm had been worse overnight with the waves hitting against the wall of the house and splashing in and down the three story staircase. She was mopping buckets of water. "Don't go near the sea, girls. It's rough today." Sheila and I visited Monkstown with lighter packs to learn about making elbow drone pipes. He directed us to Galway for uillean piper's music. "Find Seamus Ennis." The ullieann pipers and Aunt Letitia's stories set our path to explore Galway. We boarded a 10 pm train expecting to sleep all night and arrive the next morning. Surprised we arrived in Galway two and a half hours later. Now to find a hotel at midnight in a foot of snow in a small city. It was the coldest winter in forty-five years with wanting heat. We stayed bundled in down coats and sleeping bags under blankets and still could see our breath through shivers. All for the sake of art.

Because we were American, we could sit in bars, being the only women. Dark wood, peat fire smoke in the air, new spills on old spills of Guinness. Whiskey was not served until afternoon. We had our notebooks out for armor and took notes of conversations and musician's haunts. "I'd give you my farm house if you like Ireland. All the heat is by a peat fire." An older man offered. "If you're lookin' for an uilleann piper you've got to hear Seamus Ennis at Kings Head. He'll play in any pub that he enters, so keep your ear to the ground. I've got his pipes if you see him. He went home without them last night."

Tig Coili might have Tommy Keane.

Eugene Lamb at the Crane Bar or look for Liam O'Flynn or Ronana Brown, they spend a lot of time in London.

Another good bet Skeff's for Willie Clancey.

O'Connors Pub is always a good bet: just see who's there.

You can't go wrong.

We wrote in our notebooks and ordered another cup of coffee. Just then the man sitting next to us rose from his Guinness pint and in a clairvoyant voice sang a lilting limerick about a young lass in the green hills left behind in a young man's search for self. He confronted a series of impossible tasks to achieve the love of his life.

Was it an angel on our shoulder, or the luck o' the Irish, that we happened upon the legendary Seamus Ennis half way through a set. It was enough to catch the drones and trills that echoed a five thousand year old storytelling culture amidst vibrant green hills. That is how his music sounds, ancient with misty, bright green, mystical toe tapping. The "Morning Trush" composed by his father who awoke to a thrush singing every day. Seamus found the music and played it with the mist in the air and clarity of a rested lyrical repetition. We heard the magic of Eugene Lamb and Tommy Keane before flying through London to Minnesota.

~

Junior year, I was granted a January term scholarship to intern in Manhattan at *Scholastic Magazine*. My friend and I shared a room at the Biltmore Hotel across the street from Grand Central Station and several blocks from our office. Writers said they couldn't afford to go out at night, but we skimped and never stopped exploring jazz clubs, museums and visiting artists in their studios. I discovered publishing and loved it! I researched the white seal cubs of Canada being clubbed for making soft and furry keychains, coin purses and muffs. The article about depleted populations causing near extinction was written at a third-grade reading level. I didn't join the others at lunch for a week to write and rewrite for deadline. If I could get the school kids to understand, they'd tell their parents to stop buying trinkets. I was driven to find the right words to save the seal pups.

"Hundreds of letters from children came back about her Baby Seal article," my boss's letter reported to my college advisor, "letters are still arriving."

"Why are you racing through college?" my sculpting professor asked.

"Lucky-number-seven," I said. He required that I take one sculpture class to finish my major. I enrolled at the School of the Art Institute (SAIC) before May graduation. At SAIC, a few of students and I found an empty courtyard classroom with natural light and asked Professor Eldon Danhausen to teach us figure modeling. We met 9-4:00 Saturdays to learn how to sculpt the glisten in an eye and kissable lips in grey clay, splash-coat hydrocal with a surface slap, and mix and paint rubber molds. We cast in bronze in the school's foundry. Mom and Dad traveled extensively while I cared for Airdrie. I received a call for a second interview with World Book Encyclopedia where I had applied in February. By March I was drawing for the editorial department of the annual encyclopedia updates and fourteen page descriptions of new discoveries in science, art, ecology and politics.

Environmentalist Rafe Pomeranae published that the Jasons, an international scientific team, had just determined that the earth was getting warmer. National researchers dove into analytics and developed the same conclusion. A cocktail of sulfur dioxide from coal power plants, nitrogen from car exhaust and ammonia from livestock waste and fertilizers mixed with water vapors across the Midwest to rain acid on the Adirondack forests. Already half the red spruces died from the calcium sapped from their foliage. Forty-one percent of the lakes measured acidification resulting in fish having heart attacks from bursting red blood cells. Fish were eaten by humans. New research on oceans warming made larger hurricanes and tornados, denser, heavier rain and encroaching coastlines was exploding with importance. Carbon dioxide was warming the earth. We could turn it around, but we had to work fast. We had thirty years before life in earth changed dramatically. Humankind was at fault and at risk. It was called global warming.

I researched, consulted with scientists, then drew how bigger hurricanes formed from higher ocean temperatures making more powerful storms to cool the equator by transferring heat by evaporated rain falling in temperate zones. Shortages of water was, even then, causing sinkholes in Florida. Greenhouse Effect visual descriptions were constructed and photographed with three-dimensional felt to show how ozone holes allowed more sunlight into our atmosphere. Chlorofluorocarbons (CFCs) in aerosol refrigerant propellants that burned holes in the ozone were banned in the U.S.

Locally, Hazel Johnson, Chicago's "Mother of the Environmental Justice Movement," from CHA's Altgeld Gardens, became an environmental activist following the death, by lung cancer, of her husband in 1969. Her children suffered skin and respiratory ailments from Altgeld Garden's contaminated earth. Nationally, the Jasons revealed importance of the reflective white glaciers rebounding the sun's energy away from earth. The prediction was if concentrations of CO2 doubled in the atmosphere, global temperatures would rise by 2 to 3 degrees Celsius. The most devastating feature was the effect of rapid melting of the arctic ice sheets. The oceans would rise, beside a calamity of drought.

Genetically Modified Organisms (GMOs) were still experiments. DNA coding was made in painted clay and photographed to explain to readers. New breakthroughs in understanding how the plasticity of the brain could be rewired with new synapses around damaged areas were visualized for illustrators to make finished art. After a few articles, I became the go-to person for designing genetics and DNA coding explanations. GMOs were being developed and discussed for moral implications. While tomatoes where bred square for packaging, the best GMO use might be to grow rice in brackish water. The seas would rise in the Bangladesh rice fields first. We described the new science at a third-grade reading level and sent our update warnings to Bangladesh, the Arctic Poles and Iceland. Northeast trees and lakes were dying from acid rain.

Daily temperatures recorded for decades indicated global warming and scientists sounded an alarm. Gordon MacDonald advised Dwight Eisenhower on space exploration, Richard Nixon against coal, and started an Office of Carbon Dioxide. Roger Revelle advised every president since the Manhattan Project and helped the Weather Bureau establish continuous measure of atmospheric CO2 on Hawaii. He told LBJ humans have "altered the composition of the atmosphere on a global scale" through burning fossil fuel. "Future economic and political impacts would be beyond comprehension."

We wrote articles on solar and wind power, integrated and loved electric cars, wind turbines, synthetic fuels and solar panels for power. Despite Three Mile Island, nuclear was considered better than coal. Many aspects of water from acidity to unequal distribution poisoning food sources and production. Sinkholes, evaporation, the motion of water cooling the earth with rain. The possible shortage of drinking water due to weather changes. Drier areas, flooding elsewhere, melting ice, rising seas making larger and more frequent storms. Still, no one could fathom the first truly global question we'd ever had to face: how to slow the rapid heating of the earth with our dependency on fossil fuels. I biked to work. I grew a rooftop vegetable garden, purchased organic food.

Earth is between two planets. One has too much CO_2 and is too hot for life. The other is too cold. Our imbalance could go either direction, but most likely towards too hot with added CO_2. In 1979 ecology was news and not political. Everyone was on board to save our quality of life on earth. World Book told the story of sink holes and large hurricanes worldwide. We warned India, Africa, Micronesia, New Orleans, California, Nevada, Oregon and Virginia. As World Book Encyclopedia laid off 750 editorial creatives in one day, my thinking grew to express the importance of each decision being about life on earth, primarily humankind.

I remained to publish another set of updates while applying to Yale for graduate school. I chose an MFA in sculpture. At SAIC I had learned to focus my attention on the importance of an ear, or details in a hand, as a piece of the whole. Sculpture must look more like the subject than the subject itself—hyper-seeing while making rhythms in form. A few of us traveled to Italy to tour museums of Renaissance sculpture and painting in Rome, Venice and Florence. I sculpted a bronze *Reader* for the Winnetka Library, Northfield branch children's courtyard and that spring was accepted into Yale.

~

I matriculated to the 1982 Yale Master of Fine Arts class of eight sculptors, of which three were women, to sculpt nature: human, plant, and animal forms. As the first representational master's degree student in twelve years, I was terrified as I presented my first slide show to my fellow classmates. I was so nervous that I could barely speak. My fellow installation and conceptual students did not know what to say, but the look they gave me seemed to say: What rock did you crawl out from under? By this time, my sculpting heroes had expanded to include post-war Europeans sculptors, Alberto Giacometti and Marino Marini.

"I will be hiring a sculpting assistant," Erwin Hauer, Yale Professor for undergraduate sculpture studies, said at a welcome event in Yale Museum's courtyard. My ears perked up. I applied and was hired. As his assistant, I taught drawing and sculpting for undergrads on Tuesday and Thursday mornings in Hammond Hall. I studied drawing with William Bailey and art-architecture with Vincent Scully. I was off to a good start in an overwhelming place full of amazing people.

I worked with two other students, Tom and Julie, modelling for each other. One day, it was Julie's turn to sculpt my portrait in clay. Julie was moving clay around to get the proportions of my mouth and forehead in relation to my eyes.

She worked in silence. I watched, but could not see what she was sculpting. I could only see the back of the clay head. Julie wheeled the clay on a stand behind me to shape the angle of my neck in relation to my jawline.

"Take more charge of your critiques," Julie said. A visiting performance artist had thrown me off in my group crit by chiding me for sweeping up the floor of plaster chips and clay dust. "They are there to help you with your work. Ask questions to define the conversation for your needs," Julie said.

"If I sneezed, I'd be analyzed for my velocity or timidity," I said.

"I know what you mean," Julie said. "In my last painting crit, the professor told me I needed to open my eyes and look harder." My jaw dropped and I spun around. Julie's face was calm.

"The eternal optimist!" I cried out recognizing my grandmother's optimistic expression when I saw the clay portrait of me. "That is my grandmother! I didn't know I looked like her!" This was the first moment I recognized our likeness. Julie was taken aback. My surprised exclamation, out of place in this moment of quiet, raw creation, might have been confusing for her. "It looks like me and my Gramma Mac," I explained. This discovery triggered questions and longing. *Was I like her?* I didn't know anything about Gramma Mac. I didn't know anything about most women.

During my first semester, I was sculpting three full-scale women discussing art around a table when the department head, David Von Schlegel, asked if I would teach Erwin's undergraduate sculpting classes. He had been taken ill and was in the hospital. "There is no one else on campus who can teach figurative sculpture." For half of my first semester I taught Erwin's classes and became friends with the undergraduates.

I'd tell myself to calm down on the way to classes. Julie and Tom were in my class. Up until now I'd sculpted with the students, helped Erwin with building armatures, keeping the water based clay workable, the classroom and casting room clean. Erwin told the undergraduates, "The power of the image comes from convex form pushing against the space around it. The horizon of the form softens at a full roundness and hardens at darker, sharper edges defined by crisscrossing of lines like fishnet stockings, or grids on television golf course terrains. Form, extends beyond itself and into the space around it to transform the area," he'd explain in words and images. I stayed calm, arrived early, imagined where their sculpting was headed and offered ideas for a next step.

Remarkable teachers steered my figurative art in experimental directions. Erwin had studied with Marino Marini in Europe before coming to the United States. His own work was repetitive abstract architectural elements. During my first year, Garth Evans told me that talking with Alberto Giacometti was exactly like experiencing one of his sculptures. It was as if the fog of Paris were eating into the essence of an isolated man. He told me Alberto used few words, and was worn raw. Giacometti was a sparse man who survived the Great Wars. Natalie Charkov, who had taught me at Yale Norfolk, where I taught as well, had met Marino Marini in a cafe in Florence. They told me of how these sculptors art was like being in the room with the artist;

how knowing their art was like meeting them. Their stories helped me realize my charge as an art student was to find and express who seven o' nine is.

One week Alice Neel, Figurative painter, visited our class. We sat cross-legged together on the floor in the A&A common space with vertical boards filled with first year's paintings. Alice looked at each one and responded with stories or comments that might help.

My friend Gabrielle was sitting next to me. In the middle of the session she whispered, "I've got to go to the bathroom, I'll be right back. Tell me what she says." She was gone awhile. Long enough for Alice to get to talking about Gabrielle's painting.

"This artist is reaching into the past, covering the middle and making a contemporary statement. This is contemporary art. Who painted this?" Alice looked around.

"Gabrielle'll be right back," I said to keep the conversation going. "You have mentioned what I think she intends to paint, what critique would you have to share with her?" Alice stared at me long and hard. "I have a reoccurring nightmare that I wake up as an art critic." she said fiercely. "I shake and sweat when I imagine myself criticizing artwork. Whatever did you think by asking me that question?"

Just then Gabriel slipped into the spot beside me, "What just happened?"

"Here's Gabrielle, she painted that painting." I replied.

"You are a contemporary artist!" the visiting painter looked hard at Gabrielle and moved onto the next painting.

~

"So, what happened?" Ann asked about our lunch

with Richard Serra, a New York artist who sculpted with nontraditional materials such as steel, rubber and fiberglass. He visited the sculpture studios annually. "What did he say?"

Ursula von Rydingsvaard, a sculptor (whose large-scale works are influenced by nature including cedar and other forms of timber) and I had joined the others at a circular table in our school's red brick cafeteria. Second year sculptors' trays were full of plates filled with fish, broccoli, salad and cardboard boxed drinks.

"Is that chocolate milk you are drinking?" Richard Serra irascibly gestured.

"Yeah, I like chocolate milk," Pete, a classmate, said.

"I've got to get back to my bourbon in New York," Richard smirked. "You guys drink chocolate milk here."

"So, Richard..." Ursula began a calculated art dialogue of NYC artists. It was a glimpse into their world for us.

Serra turned to her and replied authoritatively, domineering and demeaning. We peered into their dialogues and their references, with a history we were trying to enter. Ursula stood up and left. To this day I wish I had left with her. The air was ripe with antagonism.

"Never make a maquette," Serra said. He now had the floor. "Never raise your sculptures above the ground on a pedestal. Never sculpt an idea less than full scale that presses into the earth."

"Wait a minute." My Irish ire was up. "Rodin put the Burghers of Calais on the ground. It is not new to put sculptures on the ground; it has been done for decades. When Rodin wanted to raise a sculpture on a pedestal, he did."

"So you know what you're talking about." Richard

looked hard at me and the conversation traveled elsewhere. During my one-on-one critique with him he had called me a reactionary. I had responded that I wanted to start with the full range of life forms to develop my direction. That weekend, I went to New York City to explore galleries and saw a new exhibit of Richard Serra's. It was of steel maquettes on pedestals.

"What did he say to Ursula?" Ann later asked. No one had a clear answer. "You've got to write him a note. Tell him you saw his work after your conversation and are glad he agrees."

"How would I get his address?" I asked.

"Send it to the gallery. They'll see that he gets it," Ann said.

My 1984 thesis exhibition was of female friends on pedestals: Doreen, Julie, Gabriella, Lena, and Laura. We completed a Yale education and tread a path for other Yale women. After I completed my Master of Fine Arts (MFA) degree, I felt confident as an artist but was concerned with how my work could make the best impact in the world.

"Julie" (c) Margot McMahon, 1960s

"Sculpted Bronze Head" (c) Margot McMahon, 1975

I traveled to Peru with friends to climb Machu Picchu. I was inspired by our five-day journey along the ancient Inca Trail with vertical walls across treacherous drops and bridges. The stone road had thousands of varieties of orchids at every turn and sometimes dipped into a tropical rain forest or rose to walled village ruins. Terraces for growing food stepped down the mountainside. The Sun Gate gave a spectacular view of the entire area. Stone storage buildings once held quinoa, corn, wheat and barley. We walked with llamas, in awe of what humankind could do. This beautiful place made me realize just how far I'd come from my days at Airdrie, when I used to admire nature from my window.

~

I returned home to Chicago and started a career in sculpting and teaching about art and nature. My artistic vision is to understand the interdependence of life forms in nature. My work includes the Chicago Tree Project, which teaches the importance of saving trees in urban nature.

When Mom's cousin showed me the family seed store after my return, I felt it was home. This is where my urge to garden originates. We are part Irish farmers. Since grade school, I had kept gardens, harvested seeds and grown vegetables from them the following year. I had grown seedlings by grow-light at Airdrie house, cleared a patch of woods by the lake for corn and planted tomatoes that were planted above nourishing alewives from the beach. I had worked at the St. Paul conservatory to understand grafting, rooting cuttings and transplanting while studying botany and hydroponics in college. In Oak Park, I grew a vertical berry-patch up the south side of my studio. I had an herb garden, leafy greens and tomatoes while training a euonymus vine into a dragon on the west studio wall. I took great pride in the pumpkin patch. The two apple trees couldn't keep our family in apple butter and pies, but I espaliered the branches and picked the fruit annually. I don't know if I have inherited my ancestors' skills, but I think I'm making them proud.

Airdrie, 2008

About the Author

Margot McMahon has received several writing awards and authored nonfiction books for adults and young adults including *The Fifth Season,* the recipient of the 2020 Mate E. Palmer First Place Book Award. An internationally-awarded sculptor, Margot lives in Chicago with her husband and visiting three grown children.

Parts of *AIRDRIE* first appeared in *If Trees Could Talk,* the second book in a trilogy about Margot's family in Chicago and Ireland. The first book, *Mac & Irene: A WWII Saga,* is based on the true story of Margot's father, Franklin "Mac" McMahon, who served as a navigator in WWII and later became an award-winning artist-reporter.

Lightning Source UK Ltd.
Milton Keynes UK
UKHW052341260822
407753UK00006B/176